Back at its birthplace: *King George V* is the most popular exhibit inside Swindon's STEAM Museum. ROBIN JONES

Written, compiled and edited: Robin Jones
Designer: Anita Tams-Waters
Sub Editor: Sarah Lawson
Production Manager: Craig Lamb
Publisher: Dan Savage

Published by
Mortons Media Group Ltd,
Media Centre, Morton Way, Horncastle, Lincolnshire
LN9 6JR.
Tel: 01507 523456

Printed by
William Gibbons and Son, Wolverhampton

Published July 2007

ISBN: 0-9552868-8-9

Media Group Ltd
Independent publishers since 1885

COVER: GWR 4-6-0 No 6000 *King George V* at Bristol Temple Mears with the 'Brunel Pullman' in June 1983. BRIAN SHARPE.

HERITAGE RAILWAY

www.heritagerailway.co.uk

DOMINE · DIRIGE · NOS ·   VIRTUTE · ET · INDUSTRIA

An oil painting by Mike Jeffries depicting Great Western Railway Churchward 4-6-0 No 4003 *Lode Star*, running along the Brunel's South Devon Railway sea wall at Dawlish in the early 1930s. The locomotive, the only survivor of its class, is one of the star exhibits in the National Railway Museum at York. COURTESY NATIONAL RAILWAY MUSEUM.

The town that *shaped a world*

Swindon today: the butt of jokes in Ricky Gervais' BBC comedy, *The Office*, in which it became the head office of Wernham Hogg paper merchants. Portrayed as a bland, soulless sea of warehouses and computer firms, Swindon housed the fictional firm's head office of the branch in which the comedy was set, on the slightly less bland, soulless Slough Trading Estate.

A town with a football club, which won the League Cup in 1969, briefly reached the dizzy heights of the Premiership and in May 2007 won promotion to League One.

A place where Honda cars are turned out by the million to award-winning Japanese designs.

Somewhere bypassed by the M4, which carries those who are in a hurry to get from west to east or vice versa.

A forgettable everyday medieval market town that grew out of a village whose name meant either "pigs' hill" or 'Sweyn's hill', after a local Saxon landowner.

A town which changed the face of the globe forever and developed transport technology years ahead of its time, paving the way for continents to be opened up to international trade, and spreading the

benefits of Britain's Industrial Revolution far and wide.

This last one is the real Swindon.

It formed the hub of Isambard Kingdom Brunel's Great Western Railway and was where a series of workshops produced groundbreaking locomotive designs, where rolling stock jumped off the drawing board on to the production line.

The town of Swindon emerged to serve a mushrooming network of lines, which stretched from Paddington to Penzance and up to west Wales, the west Midlands and the Mersey.

This network was affectionately known as God's Wonderful Railway, and was considered by many to be the best in the world.

Swindon was the town where thousands toiled to turn steel and copper into legends.

The Stars, Castles and Kings.

Not to mention the Saints, the Halls, the Granges, the Counties, the Aberdares, the prairies and the panniers.

Products that would fire the imagination decades after the steam era and the great Swindon works had come to an end.

A town synonymous with a global technological watershed, of which every resident, past, present and future has a right to be justifiably proud. ∎

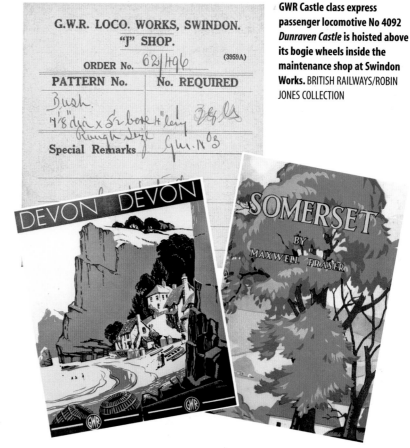

GWR Castle class express passenger locomotive No 4092 *Dunraven Castle* is hoisted above its bogie wheels inside the maintenance shop at Swindon Works. BRITISH RAILWAYS/ROBIN JONES COLLECTION

The man who made Brunel's railway work

Isambard Kingdom Brunel is rightly hailed across the globe as a genius, a man who took the technology of his day, pushed it to its limits and then a mile further. However, he was not always right. Brunel's London to Bristol railway included many engineering feats which his contemporaries were convinced could not be done, and he may have been a visionary when it came to engineering his broad gauge railway, he did not get it right when it came to locomotives.

The initial group of broad gauge locomotives ordered to his specifications proved largely unsatisfactory. A solution was needed, and fast.

It came in the form of a young engineering 'upstart', 21-year-old Daniel Gooch, who, despite his young age, was appointed as locomotive superintendent for the GWR in 1837.

Gooch was born in Bedlington, Northumberland, on 24 August 1816. Gooch met Rocket designer George Stephenson as a young boy and as soon as he was old enough he became an engineer at the locomotive factory owned by Edward Pease and George's son Robert Stephenson in Newcastle-upon-Tyne.

Gooch then found work in the foundry at Tredegar Ironworks in South Wales, but his big break came when Brunel took a gamble by giving him one of the most senior jobs in the nascent railway industry.

In doing so, Brunel proved himself to be a shrewd recruitment manager as well as

Daniel Gooch, the first GWR locomotive superintendent.

an engineering genius. His partnership with Gooch was to be a truly explosive combination, and one that would be of enormous benefit to contemporary transport and technology.

Gooch was plunged in at the deep end, having not only to sort out the mechanical problems with the motley collection of prototype locomotives that Brunel had ordered, but having to find out which ones would even haul trains.

At first, Brunel and Gooch successfully worked together on the Stephenson-designed *North Star* to improve its steaming and reduce coke consumption.

At first, *North Star* could haul no more than 16 tons at 40mph, but following modifications made by the pair, which included increasing the size of the blast pipe and ensuring that the exhaust steam was discharged up the middle of the chimney, its

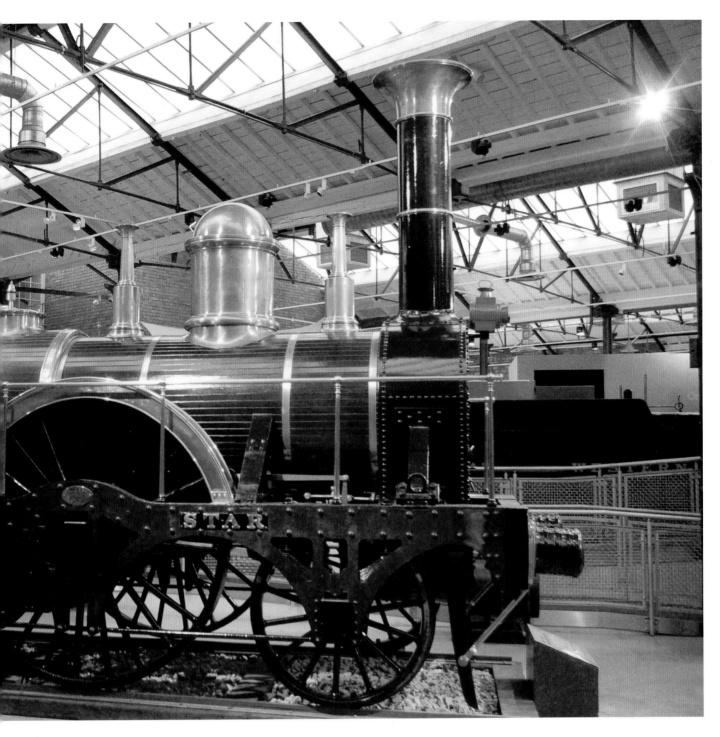

performance improved to the point whereby it could haul 40 tons at 40mph – while consuming less than a third of the quantity of coke previously used.

It was through work of this kind that Gooch, who at first shared Brunel's enthusiasm for broad gauge, became one of the finest locomotive engineers of the 19th century.

Improvement work on *North Star* and its sister locomotives led to the introduction of Gooch's Firefly class, of which 62 examples were built – by seven different outside manufacturers – in two years.

Firefly class members had a wheel arrangement of 2-2-2 – the middle '2' refers to the driving wheel – which in this case was 7ft in diameter.

Fire Fly, the first of its class, was delivered to the GWR by builder Jones, Turner and Evans of Newton-le-Willows, County Durham, on 12 March 1840.

The locomotive made its debut on 25 March, hauling two carriages carrying 40 passengers and a truck from Paddington to Reading. It reportedly covered the 30¾ miles from Twyford to Paddington in 37 mins, an average speed of 50mph, a feat without precedent in 1840.

Sister engine *Fire Ball* worked the first train from Bristol to Bath on 31 August 1840, and another of the class, *Actaeon*, played a starring role in the opening of the Bristol & Exeter Railway on 1 May 1844.

Gooch, who was also a hands-on engineman as well as a brilliant designer, was given the honour of driving the first Royal Train in 1842, hauled by his locomotive *Phlegethon*.

His Firefly class engines had chocolate-brown painted frames, green wheels with black tyres,

North Star, the Robert Stephenson locomotive which launched Brunel's broad gauge railway, on static display inside the award winning STEAM – Museum of the Great Western Railway at Swindon. ROBIN JONES

Fire Fly, the first of Daniel Gooch's Firefly class, glows in the dark, just like the glow-worm after which it was named. The setting was the 1860s Burlescombe transfer shed on the demonstration running line at Didcot Railway Centre, and the locomotive is the awardwinning modern-day replica of the original. The success of the Firefly class led to Gooch stepping up his bid for a workshop where he could supervise the construction of future designs. FRANK DUMBLETON/GREAT WESTERN SOCIETY

vermilion buffer beams – and green boilers and fireboxes.

This livery evolved into the famous Brunswick green that became the distinctive house style of the GWR empire right up until the end of steam, and which, following nationalisation in 1948, was adopted by British Railways for many of its locomotives.

In 1842, Gooch introduced the 21 members of his Sun class, also 2-2-2s, built by four different manufacturers. Class members were smaller than the Fireflys, with 6ft not 7ft driving wheels, and were less successful, being rebuilt as saddle tanks at the end of the decade, and performing much better in that guise.

Then came the 18 members of the Leo class,

2-4-0s, which were the GWR's first purpose-built goods engines. As traffic levels and loads increased, they too were converted to saddle tanks for lighter duties.

By the time the Hercules class of 0-6-0s, the first class of this wheel arrangement on the GWR, was delivered in 1842, the company had 136 engines from 11 different makers.

Gooch realised from an early stage of his employment that not only would the GWR have to have its own workshops for maintaining locomotives and rolling stock, but a factory where it could build its own, to its own exacting standards.

It is at this point that the great Swindon story began… ∎

A contemporary engraving by JC Bourne of the Great Western Railway's engine house at Swindon in 1846, the year that 2-2-2 *Great Western*, the first locomotive wholly built in the town, was turned out. GWR TRUST COLLECTION

A First Great Western High Speed Train passes the Great Western Railway workshops on the western approach to Swindon station on 2 February 2007. ROBIN JONES

WHY SWINDON?

The letter that *'made' the town*

A single letter changed Swindon from a genteel Wiltshire hilltop town into a hive of heavy industry, which through technology, would redraw much of the map of Britain and indeed the world.

The fateful note was written by Daniel Gooch, the newly-appointed 21-year-old GWR locomotive superintendent who had been asked to choose a site for the great workshops that would serve the company.

The advice of Gooch was accepted, and Swindon would never be the same again.

When he wrote to Brunel on 13 September 1840, the letter ran as follows:

My dear Sir,

According to your wish I give you my views of the best site for our principal engine establishment, and in doing so I have studied the convenience of the Great Western Railway only, but also think the same point is the only place adapted for the Cheltenham and Great Western. The point I refer to is the junction at Swindon of the two lines. The only objection I see to Swindon is the bad supply of water. There is also an apparent inequality of distance or duty for the engines to work – but which is very much equalised when the circumstances attending it are taken into account. I find the actual distances are as 76½ to 41 and the gradients are for the short distance of 41 miles a rise of 318ft or 7.75ft per mile, and for the 76½ miles a rise of 292ft or 3.8ft per mile. Swindon being the point at which these gradients change, the different gradients necessarily require a different class of engine, requiring for the Bristol end a more powerful one than for the London end.

That power can only be obtained conveniently by reducing the diameter of the driving wheels, therefore, supposing we work between Swindon and Bristol with 6ft wheels, and between Swindon and London with 7ft wheels, there will actually be very little difference between the work required of the two engines, when the additional gradients and curves, and the increased number of revolutions per mile which the small wheeled engine makes are taken into account.

It would also divide the pilot engines very nearly equally, as Reading being the first station where a pilot engine would be kept, say 36 miles, the next distance, to Swindon, would then be 41 miles, and on to Bristol another 41, and which I think would be sufficiently near for pilot engines to be constantly ready, and with this arrangement the watering stations would work very well.

Steventon, where plenty of water can be had, forming a central station between Reading and Swindon, and as our Oxford traffic comes on there I should think it likely that all trains will stop there.

A large station at Swindon would also enable us to keep our bank engines for the Wootton Bassett incline at Swindon instead of having a separate station for that purpose at the bottom of the incline and, in addition, it would at any rate be necessary to have a considerable station at Swindon to work the Cheltenham line, which would be saved if Swindon was our principal station.

It also has the great advantage of being on the side of a canal communicating with the whole of England, and by which we could get coal and coke, I should think at a moderate price. I am not sufficiently acquainted with the place to know how far we would be affected by the want of water, it might probably be collected in the neighbourhood, and as we have a great deal of side cutting they might be converted into reservoirs, and should even this fail us we have the canal.

These reasons lead me to think Swindon by far the best point we have for a Central Engine Station. From the plans and sections there appear little or no difficulties with the nature of the ground for building upon, and by placing the station somewhere, as shown in the enclosed sketch, it might be made in every respect very complete.

I have not thought of the Bristol & Exeter line in the arrangement, as it is quite possible to work it very well by engines kept at Bristol as long as they are fit for work.

In the same way we could work the additional Bath traffic, for when necessary they could always work their way to Swindon when any heavy repairs were required. The Engine House we are building at Bristol would be ample for any slight repairs that might be required during the time the engine was in working order, and that without any outlay of machinery beyond a few hundred pounds. I am not aware of any difficulties connected with Swindon more than the water.

I am, my dear Sir,
Yours very truly,
Daniel Gooch

A more romantic version of events claims that while Brunel and Gooch were surveying a valley to the north of Swindon Hill, the former either threw a stone or dropped a sandwich from a picnic lunch and declared that spot to be the new location of the works.

Brunel's GWR main line was originally planned to cut through Savernake Forest near Marlborough, but landowner the Marquess of Ailesbury was having none of it.

The line of the railway was therefore moved 20 miles to the north of the original route, passing through Swindon.

The railway needed to run near a canal, as in those earlier days it was cheaper to bring in the coal needed for the steam locomotives by barge rather than rail.

Building materials for the workshops could also be brought in by water.

The railway crossed over the North Wilts Canal, a waterway that linked the Thames & Severn Canal and the Wilts & Berks Canal.

At first, it seemed that Didcot might be chosen as the site for the works. However, over and above the considerations for locomotive changes, Gooch realised that the Wilts & Berks Canal linked Swindon to the Somerset coalfield. Drawing water for the engines from the canals was also a factor taken into consideration.

Gooch recorded in his diary: "Mr Brunel and I went to look at the ground, then only green fields, and he agreed with me as to its being the best place."

So Swindon it was. ∎

Opposite bottom left: Disused for more than a century, the North Wilts Canal, on which Brunel and Gooch decided to site Swindon Works, in now being restored to navigation, and Swindon Borough Council has shown enthusiasm for recreating an artificial waterway through the town centre once again. ROBIN JONES

Opposite bottom right: Swindon's first station, which lay at the junction of the routes to Bristol and Cheltenham, set new standards for passenger comfort when it opened. ILLUSTRATED LONDON NEWS/ BRUNEL 200

History of the
Great Western Railway

SPEED TO THE WEST
CORNWALL DEVON SOMERSET WALES

It was in 1800 that the first scheme for a railway linking Bristol to London – using horses to pull the trains – was drawn up by Dr John Anderson.

Two schemes in the mid-1820s, when steam traction was still viewed with scepticism in many quarters, quickly came to nothing.

However, following the Rainhill Trials of 1829, won by George Stephenson's *Rocket*, and the subsequent opening of Liverpool & Manchester Railway, it was clear to all that steam haulage was the future.

In 1832, four Bristol businessmen, John and William Harford, Thomas Guppy and George Jones, looked again at the prospect of a rail link to the capital. City merchants saw the urgency to maintain the position of Bristol as the second port in the country and the chief one for American trade in the face of growing competition from Liverpool developing its own rail connection with London.

The next year, Nicholas Roch, a member of the Bristol Docks Committee, was asked to find an engineer for the job.

He approached his young friend Isambard Kingdom Brunel, the great engineer to be, whose work on the city harbour and whose plans for a suspension bridge to cross the Avon Gorge at Clifton had won a competition in 1831, the year that construction started (although it was not to be completed until 1864, five years after his death).

Isambard Brunel was born on 9 April 1806 in Portsmouth and was educated in both England and France. His father Marc was a French engineer who had fled France during the Revolution and was working on block-making equipment for the Portsmouth Block Mills at the time.

At 14 Isambard was sent to France to be educated at the Lycée Henri-Quatre in Paris and the University of Caen in Normandy, and when he returned to England, he went to work for his father.

Isambard Brunel's first notable achievement was the part he played in his father Marc's greatest achievement, the Thames Tunnel, which ran from Rotherhithe to Wapping, and was completed in 1843.

The first major sub-river tunnel, it succeeded where

Firefly class 2-2-2 broad gauge locomotive *Tiger* was a member of Daniel Gooch's class of locomotives which amazed his generation with its speed and power. It was built by Sharp Roberts & Co of Manchester in 1840, but rebuilt at Swindon with longer frames and a new boiler and firebox in November 1864. It is pictured outside Swindon Works. BROAD GAUGE SOCIETY

other attempts had failed, thanks to Marc Brunel's tunnelling shield, which protected workers from collapses by placing them within a protective casing. It was hailed as one of the wonders of the world, and crowds flocked to walk through it: today, it is a relatively obscure part of the London Underground network.

When invited to enter a 'contest' with several rivals to find out who could build the London to Bristol railway for the cheapest price, Isambard Brunel replied with disdain.

He told the scheme's backers that he would only survey a route that would be the best, not the cheapest – and gambled with his reputation, largely established through his work on the Thames Tunnel. He won.

Told to survey the route within a month, Brunel set

out on horseback, drew up his route, and saw the project – initial estimated cost £2,800,000 - formally launched at Bristol Guildhall on 30 July 1833.

The first joint meeting of the 'London & Bristol Railroad' was held at the offices of Gibbs & Sons in Lime Street in London on 22 August 1833, but by the time the prospectus was issued, the name had been changed to the Great Western Railway – reportedly at Brunel's behest.

After first being rejected by the House of Lords on 25 July 1834, the company revised the scheme and the enabling Parliamentary Bill received Royal Assent on 31 August 1835. Work began within a month, and Brunel, appointed its engineer at the age of 27, was on the road to becoming a household name.

Whereby most contemporary railway projects conformed to the 'Stephenson gauge' of 4ft 8½in

'The Flying Dutchman' was in broad gauge days the world's fastest train. This view dates from Edwardian times, with the train hauled by an unidentified 4-4-0. ROBIN JONES COLLECTION

between the rails (a measurement said to derive from the average space between the wheels of coal carts in the north-east), Brunel decided to push technology to the limits, and opted for a radical and controversial 7ft 0¼in gauge.

Brunel told the GWR directors that there would be advantages in reducing the centre of gravity of rolling stock by mounting coach and wagon bodies between the wheels rather than above them. Furthermore, a wider gauge would offer bigger and more powerful locomotives and carriages, as well as wagons with a greater capacity.

However, he acknowledged that it would be impossible for GWR trains to run over other lines built to 4ft 8½in gauge, or what is today known as 'standard gauge'.

Brunel did not want to standardise with everyone else. He wanted to be the best – and there are many who believe today that had the world opted for his broad gauge, railways would play a far bigger role in our modern transport system.

The broad gauge locomotive *North Star*, built by Robert Stephenson at Newcastle-upon-Tyne, was delivered to the GWR and in May 1838, hauled the first passenger train over the first section of 24 miles from Paddington to Maidenhead on 4 June that year.

The GWR's first engine driver was Jim Hurst, who was also thought to have been its first waged employee.

He joined in August 1837 at the age of 26, having approached GWR locomotive superintendent Daniel Gooch for a job, after riding with him on the footplate of locomotives at Vulcan Works where he was previously employed.

Beginning with the inaugural daily services from Paddington to Taplow, then known as Maidenhead, Hurst, who had never attended school and who had

begun work as a cotton handloom weaver in his native Lancashire at the age of nine, eventually drove trains all over the GWR system. A somewhat volatile character, he was sacked in June 1856 for fighting with a porter, but was reinstated shortly afterwards, possibly after intervention from Gooch. Hurst retired in May 1876 and died in August 1892.

It was not until June 1841 that the completed

Castle class No 5095 *Barbury Castle* heads the 5.30pm from Newton Abbot to Kingswear on 24 April 1961. PETER GRAY

GWR TRUST COLLECTION

Another major innovation was the commissioning by the GWR of the world's first commercial telegraph line, running for 13 miles from Paddington station, the London terminus, to West Drayton, which came into operation on 9 April 1839.

The 1840s were the great period of what became known as Railway Mania, with speculators rushing to jump on the high-speed transport bandwagon with a plethora of schemes ranging from the brilliant to the delusional.

The GWR began expanding its empire either by operating trains on lines big and small, on behalf of new companies without the wherewithal to build and service their own locomotives and carriage stock, or by absorption of other companies.

The Bristol route was extended to Exeter by the opening, in 1844, of the initially independent Bristol & Exeter Railway, again with Brunel as its engineer, and thereon to Plymouth via his South Devon Railway and on to Penzance via the Cornwall Railway, all built to broad gauge.

Queen Victoria became the first reigning monarch to travel by train when she made her first journey, between Slough and London, on the GWR on 13 June 1842.

In 1843, the GWR bought the Cheltenham and Great Western Union Railway, which took broad gauge to Gloucester, where passengers were forced to change trains. Goods had to be manhandled from Brunel's broad gauge trucks and wagons to the standard gauge counterparts of the Birmingham & Gloucester Railway, leading to much controversy and lampooning of his empire and the need for a universal gauge.

In 1846, the Gauge Commission recommended that all future lines should be built to 4ft 8½in gauge, but the GWR was allowed to continue with the broad gauge within its territory.

The Birmingham & Oxford Junction Railway, Berks and Hants Railway, the Birmingham, Wolverhampton & Dudley Railway, Oxford, Worcester & Wolverhampton Railway, the Oxford & Rugby Railway, the South Wales Railway, the Shrewsbury & Birmingham Railway, the Wilts, Somerset and Weymouth Railway, the West Midlands Railway, the Shrewsbury & Chester Railway and the aforementioned West Country concerns became part and parcel of Brunel's sprawling empire.

Several of the acquisitions had been built to standard gauge, and rather than convert them to 7ft 0¼in in the face of worsening hostility (the Royal Commission on Railways recommended in 1857 that no more broad gauge lines should be built), the GWR laid mixed gauge tracks, so trains of both sizes could run on the same line.

Brunel died from a stroke in 1859, shortly after seeing his magnificent tubular steel Royal Albert Bridge at Saltash, linking the South Devon and Cornwall railways, opened. A genius who always had

GWR line from Bristol to London, a distance of 118 miles and in part nicknamed 'Brunel's billiard table' because of its smoothness, was completed at a cost of £6,500,000, more than twice the original estimate, with breathtaking features such as Sonning Cutting, the gravity-defying elliptical-arched bridge at Maidenhead, and Box Tunnel. In 1999, the complete route was nominated for consideration as a World Heritage Site, like the Taj Mahal and the Great Barrier Reef, such is its technological and cultural importance.

Swindon station was opened into 1842 and went straight into the history books by installing the first-ever public railway refreshment rooms. They offered the only refreshments available on the railway between Bristol and London, but complaints about the quality of the food and drink served were commonplace.

Messrs. J&C Rigby had built the station at its own expense, in return for the right to operate the refreshment rooms on the ground floor and a hotel on the upper ones, under an agreement with the railway that all trains passing through would stop for 10 minutes. The arrangement did not work well and in 1895 the GWR bought back the lease.

Swindon Works

several major projects 'on the go', it is said that exhaustive work on his greatest steamship project, the *SS Great Britain*, brought about his premature demise.

Brunel's achievements, the greatest of which was probably the building of the GWR, would never be forgotten, and in a television poll he was voted the second greatest Briton of all time, behind Sir Winston Churchill. Not bad for a man who was half French. In 2006, celebrations to mark the bicentenary of his birth led to major revaluations of many of his lesser-known works.

In 1861, the mixed gauge reached Paddington, the headquarters of the GWR, and it was clear that the writing was on the wall for broad gauge. In 1866, a programme of converting broad gauge routes to standard gauge begun north of Oxford. Large-scale conversions began in 1872, the year that the mixed gauge reached Swindon.

Finally, on 21 May 1892, the 177-mile route from Paddington to Penzance was converted, bringing down the final curtain on Brunel's broad gauge and rendering its locomotives and rolling stock fit for nothing but the scrapyard.

At the same time, the GWR did much to upgrade its services, providing restaurant cars, improved conditions for third-class passengers, and steam heating of trains.

In 1890, all GWR trains began to carry third class passengers, who, before that had been restricted to certain trains.

Two years later, the GWR introduced 'all-corridor' trains, but only the guard had access throughout to ensure that second- and third-class passengers did not disturb their first-class counterparts! Soon, the railway's name became a trademark synonymous with luxury, style and comfort.

The company had also begun shortening its routes wherever possible to speed up services and make train travel more attractive. In 1886, the GWR opened the Severn Tunnel to shorten the route between London and South Wales. At four miles 628 yards, it is Britain's longest railway tunnel, Channel Tunnel apart.

Another first had come in 1855, when the GWR ran the country's first special postal train, between London and Bristol.

As we shall see, a succession of record-breaking steam locomotives were built for the GWR system, from its broad gauge days right up into the middle of the 20th century. Perhaps most famously of all, in 1904 when City class 4-4-0 No 3440 *City of Truro*, albeit unofficially, was said to have become the first in the world to break the 100mph barrier, on Wellington Bank in Somerset, when taking the 'Ocean Mails Special' from Plymouth to Paddington, and much more was to come in the decades that followed.

In 1908, the first British Pacific locomotive, with a wheel arrangement of 4-6-2, was built by the GWR, and named *The Great Bear*.

When WWI broke out, Britain's major railways were placed under government control, but Whitehall stopped short of heeding calls for the 'nationalisation' to be made permanent.

Instead, most railway companies were herded into four large groups, thereafter nicknamed the 'Big Four'.

At the Grouping, which took place on 1 January 1923, the GWR amalgamated with more companies, including the Barry Railway, the Cambrian Railways, the Cardiff Railway, the Rhymney Railway, the Alexandra (Newport & South Wales) Docks and Railway Company, and the Taff Vale Railway, while absorbing their subsidiaries.

Taking on board so many of the major freight

Brunel's Royal Albert Bridge across the Tamar into Cornwall was opened in 1859, completing the rail link from Paddington to Penzance, and eventually opening up the delectable duchy to Swindon-built classics. On 7 April 2007, two of them, King 4-6-0 No 6024 *King Edward I* and Castle 4-6-0 No 5051 *Earl Bathurst* take the 'Great Britain' railtour into Devon. BRIAN SHARPE

Farmer John Arkell opened his steam brewery at Swindon in 1843, the same year as Brunel's works opened. An entrepreneur, he saw the vast potential for ale sales with the influx of workers in the years ahead. This 1980s beermat recalls the Great Western Railway pioneer locomotive North Star. ROBIN JONES COLLECTION

Above: Preserved GWR diesel railcar No 4, a type later built at Swindon, on display at the town's STEAM museum. ROBIN JONES

Above right: In its final years, the Great Western Railway began looking to the years when steam would be obsolete, and in 1946 ordered a gas turbine locomotive. No 18000, from the Swiss firm of Brown Boveri. It was delivered in 1951, but the concept was quickly overtaken by diesel and electric traction in British Railways days. No 18000 is now a static exhibit at The Railway Age in Crewe. FRED KERR

routes in the South Wales' coalfield was at first seen as a major boost for the fortunes of the GWR shareholders, but in the decade that followed, traffic declined significantly as the use of coal as a naval fuel declined – leaving the railway as the largest single user of Welsh coal.

One of the 33 concerns that were merged into the GWR group under the provisions of the Railways Act 1921 was the 'other' rail route to Swindon, the Midland & South Western Junction Railway, which had been formed in 1884 by the amalgamation of the Swindon, Marlborough & Andover Railway and the Swindon & Cheltenham Extension Railway. The route, which ran from Andoversford near Cheltenham to Andover in Hampshire, had been operated by the GWR's rivals the Midland Railway and the London & South Western Railway.

Some regard the 1920s as the greatest period in the history of the GWR, if only for the superb express locomotives such as the Castles and Kings, which were turned out by chief mechanical engineer Charles Benjamin Collett. At first they beat all comers, but eventually the London, Midland & Scottish Railway and the London & North Eastern Railway turned out

faster and more powerful locomotives as part of their competition for the Anglo-Scottish market.

Nonetheless, the GWR remained in relatively good financial health despite the depression of the 1930s. In fact, in 1932 it boasted the world's fastest train, with Castle class 4-6-0 No 5006 *Tregenna Castle* running from Swindon to Paddington with the 'Cheltenham Spa Express' in 57 minutes.

Just as Brunel had hoped to continue his railway from Bristol to North America via a series of steamships, the Great Western (launched in 1837 by the company's directors even though the railway had not been opened) and the *SS Great Britain*, so the GWR looked beyond steel wheels to other modes of transport in the 20th century.

In 1903, the GWR introduced its own bus services from Helston to The Lizard, and in 1933 launched its own air service linking Cardiff, Teignmouth, Torquay and Plymouth.

The following year, it launched diesel railcars, heralding the type of passenger train most commonplace on Britain's national network today.

The company attained another world first – that of the longest daily non-stop train anywhere, the 'Cornish Riviera Express' from Paddington to Penzance.

During WWII, the railways were again brought under the direct control of the Government, and before the conflict ended, a Labour government was in place to nationalise them – this time for good.

On 1 January 1948, the GWR itself was absorbed – into the new national conglomerate that was British Railways, and a new dawn began as the Swindon empire became its Western Region. History would show that the GWR would not surrender its independence that easily.

Perhaps the GWR had the last laugh, for one of its last directors, the Conservative MP Harold Macmillan, helped Winston Churchill defeat the Labour government in the 1951 general election, and went on to become Prime Minister himself in 1957.

He had never had it so good, but then, over the past century, neither had the GWR – with a beating heart in the form of Swindon's workshops to turn out the locomotives, carriages and wagons that became the envy of the world.

Therein lies the real story of the GWR empire. ■

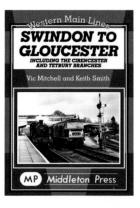
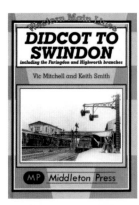
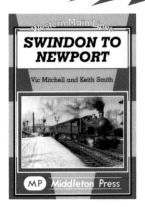
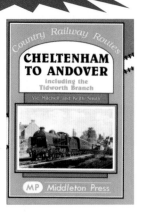

An aerial view of Swindon Works and station on 30 August 1938. GWR TRUST COLLECTION

The story of *Swindon Works*

In the spring of 1841, building of the new works at Swindon started, along with the provision of housing for the workforce, most of which would move to the town from outside Wiltshire.

The first building at Swindon Works, the locomotive repair shed, was completed that year using contract labour, and machinery was installed within it by 1842.

The London firm of Messrs. J&C Rigby, which built and operated the refreshment rooms at Swindon station, constructed 300 cottages along with a railway

hotel, and, as the GWR was trying to save money, agreed to reimbursement from tenants' rents.

The estate comprising the cottages was known as New Swindon.

In January 1843, six months after the town's station had opened, works' manager Archibald Sturrock declared the workshops to be in full operation.

The works were sited half a mile to the west of the station, and included an engine depot built parallel to the main running line and which was capable of housing 100 locomotives.

A 1940s view of locomotives under construction at Swindon. GWR

At right angles to it stood the engine house, which could accommodate up to 36 engines undergoing repairs and maintenance at any one time.

There were smaller workshops for use by pattern makers, wheel turners, millwrights, toolmakers and copper smiths.

Repairs began in 1843, with at the outset 200 men being employed, quickly rising to 423 in the same year.

Adjoining the north side of the engine house was the erecting house, where 18 locomotives could be built simultaneously.

The first new locomotive, *Premier*, an 0-6-0 freight locomotive and one of a class of 12, emerged from the works in February 1846. Its boiler was purchased from an outside manufacturer, and so it cannot be considered the first locomotive to be built entirely at Swindon, but it does show that a decision had been made to start building engines there.

Because of the pressure on the GWR to justify its use of broad gauge, in 1846 the company ordered Gooch to produce a "colossal locomotive working with all speed".

Gooch, by then installed as locomotive superintendent, again seized the opportunity, and within 13 weeks, an all-Swindon-built engine

emerged from the works – and was appropriately named *Great Western*.

First built as a 2-2-2, on 1 June 1846 *Great Western* covered the 194-mile journey from Paddington to Exeter with a train of unrecorded weight in 208 mins, and returned in 211 mins. Brunel was on board the train, along with GWR chairman Charles Russell.

After the leading axle fractured in service at Shrivenham, in Oxfordshire, *Great Western* was converted, or rather 'fine tuned' to a 4-2-2.

Its success made it the prototype of all broad gauge express passenger locomotives, and the Swindon order book was finally and firmly opened.

It was on 29 April 1847 that *Iron Duke*, the first of a legendary class bearing the same name, made its trial trip from Swindon Works. Twenty-two members of the class were built at Swindon, the most famous being *Lord of the Isles*, which went on display at the 1851 Great Exhibition in Crystal Palace.

By 1848, the works' floorspace had been doubled and by 1851, the works was employing more 2000 men and turning out a locomotive a week.

A slump in 1849 saw the workforce cut to 600, but the company recovered quickly; its financial stability meant it could pay its workers much higher wages

Above: 9A 1940s aerial view of the locomotive works. GWR

Above right: Castle class No 5094 *Tretower Castle* receives attention inside the works in January 1958. JOHN STRETTON COLLECTION

than their counterparts working on the land in the area.

Between 1846 and 1858, 39 passenger and 109 goods locomotives were built for the GWR broad gauge network, and 24 engines – the first in 1855 – to 4ft 8½in gauge for other companies.

In 1860, the GWR ordered a rolling mill to be built at Swindon to work up worn or damaged rails into new ones.

The opening of the rolling mill created many more jobs and attracted huge numbers of workers from South Wales, creating a large Welsh community in the booming town.

The rolling mill was not a huge success, but by the mid-1860s, the country was undergoing a nationwide trade boom and the demand for new railway rolling stock was soaring.

In 1865, Swindon had to turn away 18 orders for new engines so it could cope with the 30 that had been accepted.

The building of additional locomotives and rolling stock rolling stock was delegated to newer workshops

A Castle boiler being lowered on to its frame during construction. GWR

at Wolverhampton (which produced 800 standard gauge locomotives up to 1908), Worcester and Saltney near Chester, although the GWR concentrated most of the work at Swindon.

Over and above locomotive building, from 1850 standardised goods wagons were produced and in 1868, Swindon became the central GWR workshop for the construction of carriages and wagons as well as engines. That year, a new carriage and wagon works, which had originally been earmarked for Oxford, was built at Swindon on land north of the station, and 13 miles of additional sidings were laid.

The workforce population soared, as all sorts of skilled craftsmen were taken on: bodymakers, wagon builders, coach trimmers and painters. The first royal saloon was built in 1874.

In 1875, Swindon's boiler- and tender-making shops were opened. Not only did they provide components for locomotives but also parts for marine engines for use in the GWR's fleet of barges and ships.

With the demise of broad gauge in 1892, all locomotives and rolling stock were recalled to Swindon.

Broad gauge engines, carriages and wagons were amassed on a series of specially laid tracks.

Those that could be converted to 4ft 8½in gauge were adapted appropriately: the others were scrapped.

By the turn of the century, the works was employing around three quarters of Swindon's entire workforce.

Much heavier locomotives were built during the reign of George Jackson Churchward, who was appointed assistant chief superintendent in 1897, being promoted to locomotive superintendent in 1902. They began with his City class of 4-4-0s, which were followed by the County class, and a succession of four-cylinder 4-6-0s, and the company's only 4-6-2, *The Great Bear*.

Churchward's successor, Charles Benjamin Collett, chief mechanical engineer from 1921 to 1941, made major improvements in the works' boiler-making capacity, and also improved facilities for working heavy gauge sheet metal.

Under him, in 1927, the most powerful GWR locomotive type of all, the 4-6-0 King class was introduced, the first being No 6000 *King George V*.

Built at Swindon, the Kings, a development of the Castle class of 1923, became the flagship of the GWR fleet.

The works continued to swallow up more greenfield areas, as more revolutionary locomotive types were being batch built. In Collett's day, 14,000 people were employed at Swindon Works. Its main locomotive fabrication workshop, the A Shop was, at 11¼ acres, one of the largest covered areas in the world when it opened in 1920.

In April 1924, Collett had the honour of welcoming King George V and his wife Queen Mary to the works.

Frederick William Hawksworth replaced Collett in 1941, and his tenure lasted eight years.

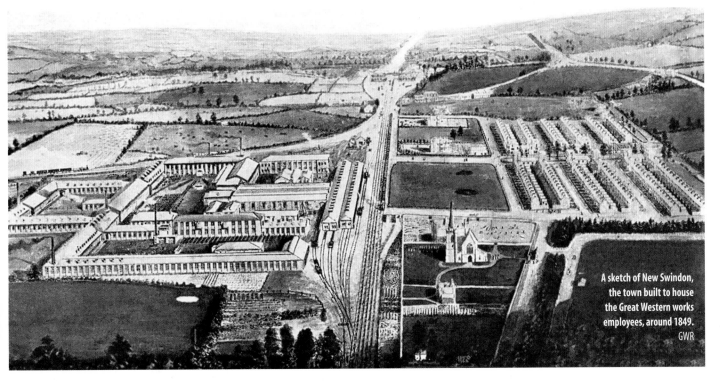

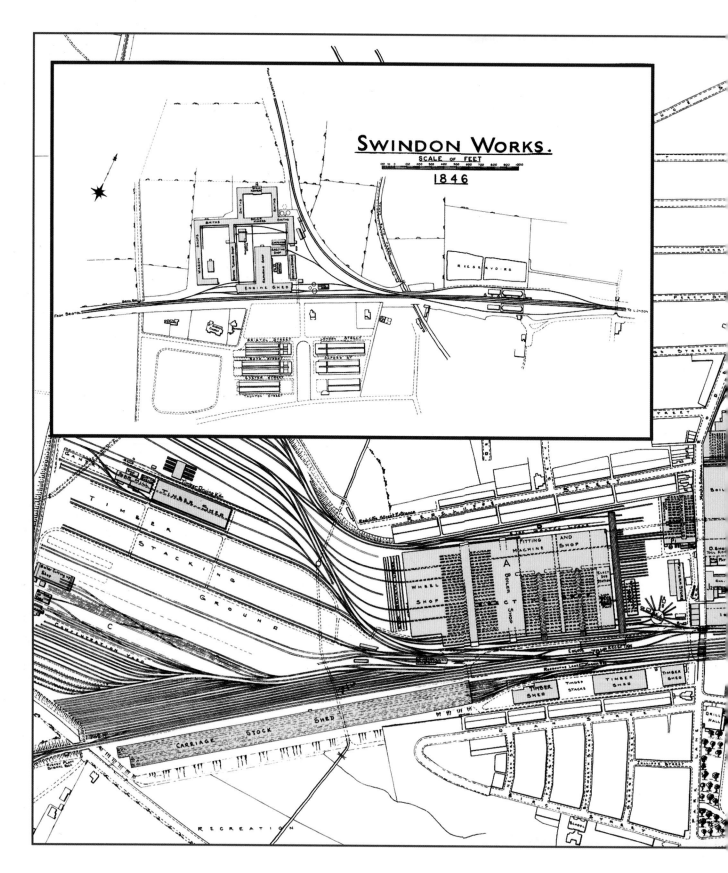

In the final year of GWR independence, the works was still turning out 60 engines a year.

Nationalisation, and the transformation of the GWR into British Railways' Western Region, brought many new opportunities for Swindon. Hawksworth's modified version of Collett's Hall 4-6-0s and his pannier tanks were still turned out, while around 200 examples of the new Standard locomotive types designed for British Railways were built there.

On 15 November 1950, HRH Princess Elizabeth visited Swindon Works and named the last Castle 4-6-0 to be built, No 7037 *Swindon*.

The writing may have been on the wall, however, with the publication in 1955 of the British Railways Modernisation Plan, which, in short, called for the total replacement of steam haulage by diesel and electric traction.

It was at Swindon that the first main line diesel

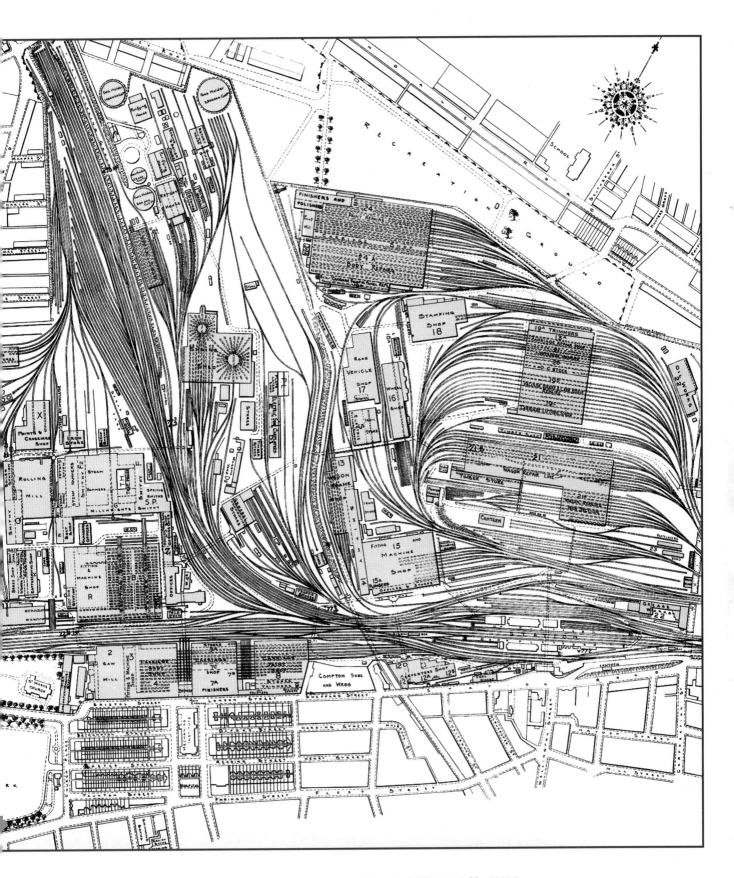

hydraulic locomotive for Britain was turned out in 1957. Over the next five years, the Western Region's most famous classes, the Westerns and the Warships, emerged from Swindon.

Building diesel locomotives at the works, however, was nothing new: six diesel-electric 0-6-0 shunters had been outshopped there in 1948.

Three years later, the works had the honour of producing the last British Railways' steam locomotive,

in the form of Standard 9F 2-10-0 No 92220 *Evening Star*.

Building of new locomotives at Swindon for the national network, steam or diesel, came to an end in 1962 following a major reorganisation under the British Transport Commission's National Workshops Plan.

The locomotive section of Swindon Works was all but entirely rebuilt. The end result was that the works

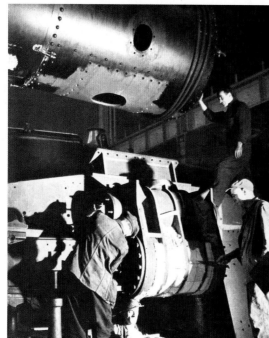

was left with the responsibility of repairing and modifying the existing locomotive fleet, mainly the diesel hydraulic types that were unique to the Western Region, while carriage and wagon work continued, although the original carriage and wagon workshop was sold.

A Works Training School was built in 1962 on the far side of the main line to the works, and accommodated 112 apprentices.

The infamous Beeching Axe was wielded in 1963. Dr Richard Beeching had been given the remit to close unprofitable and unsustainable branch lines throughout the country, a process that to some extent had already been underway for many years both in the Western Region and elsewhere.

As more lines closed, fewer locomotives and less stock were needed, and so the input into Swindon Works was reduced.

The newly formed British Rail Engineering Ltd (BREL) took over the works from 1 January 1970, and in the decade that followed, Swindon was awarded a major proportion of a contract for overhauling British Rail's ageing diesel multiple-unit fleet.

In 1978, Swindon Works was awarded a lucrative contract to carry out the major refurbishment of the Southern Region's Class 411/412 CEP/BEP electric multiple-unit fleet, and A Shop was converted for the purpose.

Locomotive building returned to Swindon in 1980 when 20m gauge 0-8-0 diesel hydraulic shunters were built for Kenya Railways.

Meanwhile, steam had not vanished altogether. While 11 August 1968 is widely quoted as the day when the last steam train – an enthusiasts' charter, the 'Fifteen Guinea Special' – ran in north-west England, British Rail had one steam line left.

It was the 1ft 11½in gauge Vale of Rheidol Railway, running between Aberystwyth and Devil's Bridge in central Wales, and which ran three 2-6-2 tank engines built by the GWR in 1923-24. The locomotives would return to Swindon for maintenance and overhaul in A Shop.

The scenes at the end of broad gauge in 1892 were repeated regularly at Swindon during most of the works' BREL years.

Most of the Western Region diesel hydraulics were scrapped there, and from the mid-70s onwards, a department was devoted solely to scrapping locomotives, carriages and wagons from all across the national network. More than a century after Brunel and Gooch had made Swindon a centre of excellence for transport technology, it had become a huge railway graveyard.

The town was left dumbstruck in the summer of 1985 when BREL announced that the whole of Swindon Works would close from the middle of the following year.

BREL quoted declining order books and the lack of contracts from its main customer, British Rail. As a result, work practices had to be rationalised, leading to inevitable closures. ∎

A blueprint for the NHS?

It was not only in transport technology that the GWR was years ahead of its time. The concern Brunel, Gooch and the company's directors showed for the men who worked for them was, in their day, as radical as their engineering exploits. They lived in an age when young children worked in factories and mines, when conditions for the working classes living in the new conurbations spawned by the Industrial Revolution were often poor and life expectancy for workers in certain trades, such as slate mining, was notoriously short.

Gooch oversaw the building of a model village for his workers. Concerned for the moral and physical welfare of the men under him, he brought in a works' doctor who stayed in free lodgings.

The workers' village was called New Swindon and is today known as the Railway Village. At the time it was separate from Old Swindon, but as the booming railway brought waves of prosperity and new inhabitants to the town, the two merged into one.

The Railway Village, one of the earliest examples of planned industrial housing in Britain, was designed by Sir Matthew Digby Wyatt, architect of Paddington station. It comprised 300 limestone-built terraced cottages, each with its own small garden, which sit in a series of six tree-lined wide streets – each named after nearby GWR stations.

Much of the stone for the houses came from the

The Mechanics Institute in the 1920s. GWR

excavations of Box Tunnel and the larger residences were allocated to under-managers and foremen.

The village had three pubs and a church – St Mark's, which was built largely through public subscription – and a graveyard where generations of local railwaymen found their final resting place within a stone's throw of Brunel's main line.

Next to the church was a school, built in 1845 for the children of GWR employees. Weekly fees were charged for the first four children of a family, but any more could go free.

The planners provided a $10\frac{1}{2}$ acre park for the recreation of GWR workers and their families. As well as regular band concerts, fetes and cricket matches were held there: once, the legendary WG Grace played on the pitch, and later Baden Powell reviewed his troops of Boy Scouts there.

At the heart of the village was the Mechanics' Institute, a building of great national importance – though today it lies derelict as debates about its future use continue.

Opened on 1 May 1855, it was funded by Gooch and works' manager Minard Christian Rea's New Swindon Improvement Company, with the aim of providing evening classes for manual workers and their families.

The Institute also had a theatre and stage, baths and coffee rooms. It served as a community centre, long before local authorities saw the need for such establishments to provide a focus for community life.

A marketplace was provided in the Railway Village, ensuring that workers could obtain a supply of fresh produce at reasonable prices, and a library, which had just 130 volumes in March 1844, predated the first council library in Britain that opened in Salford in 1852.

A GWR Medical Fund Society was established and financed a cottage hospital.

In return for a small weekly deduction from their wages, employees and their families were entitled to a complete medical service, subsidised by the GWR.

It provided doctors' surgeries, dental and eye clinics and a casualty department, as well as facilities for every branch of health care, from chiropody to the provision of artificial limbs.

This fund was a world first and would, a century

later, become the model for the cradle-to-grave care ideals of Aneurin Bevan when he drew up his blueprint for the National Heath Service.

If that is so, the railway aside, Britain indeed has much to thank Swindon for.

Other amenities that appeared in and around the Railway Village were washing baths, a savings bank, and a provident fund to support those who found themselves unable to work through sickness.

When such amenities are today taken for granted, it is easy to forget that in mid-19th century Britain, when slavery was still legal in parts of the USA, that such things were considered unheard-of luxuries by a large proportion of the population.

Unlike contemporary Victorian housing for manual workers in the rest of Britain, much of which quickly degenerated into back-to-back slums, the Railway Village is still thriving today.

With the shrinking of the workforce in the 1960s, Swindon Borough Council bought most of the cottages in the village and shortly afterwards they received the protection of listed building status.

The council began to modernise the properties in 1969, while at the same time carefully preserving their character and appearance.

One cottage, 34 Faringdon Road, was returned to its late Victorian condition both inside and out, and opened as the Railway Village Museum. Its kitchen includes; the original range and copper, a brown glazed sink, a tin bath and mangle, a living room laid

out ready for tea, a parlour with table, chairs and sideboard, and three bedrooms with iron and brass bedsteads.

The works may have closed, but the village built to serve them remains.

Was it coincidence that an employer, which displayed such concern for the well-being of each and every one of its employees, went on to became a byword for achievement and excellence in its main sphere of activity, the railways? ■

The National Railway Museum's replica of the original *Iron Duke* on the broad gauge demonstration line at York. NRM

The age of the *Iron Dukes*

Lightning, one of the acclaimed Iron Duke class, was also one of the first steam locomotives to be built at Swindon Works. GWR

Daniel Gooch set the standard at Swindon in more ways than one. Even before the first sod had been cut to make way for the great works, he insisted on standardisation of parts as far as his locomotive designs were concerned.

Broadly speaking, components from one class of locomotive could be exchanged with those of another, paving the way for economies of scale when it came to building, maintenance and repairs.

As we will see, this policy of interchangeable parts had proud implications for Swindon products, right up to the present day.

The first class of engines to be built entirely at Swindon were the Princes, six 2-2-2 locomotives designed for passenger work, all with 7ft driving wheels, apart from the semi-experimental *Witch*; it had a 7ft 6in version, built for passenger work.

The Princes were, in effect, stopgaps for the Paddington-Exeter service, and were quickly replaced, once Gooch had refined his Iron Duke 4-2-2 class – 29 members, all with 8ft driving wheels – for the purpose. The Princes entered service between August 1846 and March 1847, and were later seconded to the Oxford and Birmingham routes. They were withdrawn in 1870 with an average of 600,000 miles on the clock.

The Iron Dukes, however, became the flagship of Brunel's broad gauge, and an early testament to the quality of Swindon products.

As with *Fire Fly*, the GWR broad gauge classes took their names from the first to be built. The first of the new 4-2-2s to be turned out, which outshopped from Swindon in April 1847, was called *Iron Duke* because its trial run took place on 29 April, birthday of the Duke of Wellington.

Swindon built 22 Iron Dukes between then and 1851, while Rothwell and Co of Bolton supplied another seven in 1854-55.

In the mid-19th century, they represented transport technology at its finest. One of the class, *Great Britain*, maintained average speeds of 67mph on runs from London to Didcot in 1848, while the class boasted an estimated top speed of about 80mph.

Iron Dukes were used to haul the 'Flying Dutchman' express train from Paddington to Exeter. For several decades it was the fastest train in the world. In 1852 the daily service was achieved with an average speed of 53mph, with the 'billiard table' section between London and Swindon covered at an average of 59mph.

Class doyen *Iron Duke*, which spent most of its working life allocated to the Westbourne Park (Paddington) shed, was withdrawn in August 1873 after covering 607,412 miles in service. Sister locomotive *Lightning* set the record for class mileage, 816,601 prior to withdrawal in 1878.

Lord of the Isles, a hereditary title given to the eldest son of the British monarch, was the most famous engine of the class, recording nearly 800,000 miles in 30 years' service and all with its original boiler. It originally carried the name *Charles Russell* in honour of the GWR director.

In 1852 *Lord of the Isles* hauled the director's inspection train from Paddington to Birmingham but was involved in a collision at Aynho, in Northamptonshire, en route.

Following withdrawal, and despite the demise of the broad gauge, *Lord of the Isles* was exhibited at Edinburgh in 1890, Chicago in 1893, and Earls Court, London in 1897.

The GWR had decided to preserve it at Swindon, but disgracefully, in January 1906, it was cut up to free up floorspace.

More classes appeared from Swindon Works in fairly rapid succession, with six Pyracmon class 0-6-0 freight locomotives, slightly bigger than the Premiers, turned out in 1847. The eight members of the Caesar class of freight 0-6-0s, a development of the Pyracmons, followed in 1851.

The biggest class of all in terms of locomotive numbers was Gooch's Standard Goods, or Ariadne class.

A total of 102 were built at Swindon in the 11 years from 1852, and they proved so successful that examples survived right up to the end of broad gauge in 1892. Class member *Europa* was the last 7ft 0¼in

Dawn near Reading, showing a westbound train around 1870.
ELTON COLLECTION: IRONBRIDGE GORGE MUSEUM TRUST

gauge locomotive to work out of Plymouth, departing for Swindon on 21 May 1892.

Gooch also designed many successful locomotives for other broad gauge lines, including the Bristol & Exeter Railway, the South Devon Railway, the Cornwall Railway and the Vale of Neath Railway.

To tackle the notorious South Devon banks between Exeter and Plymouth, he designed the Corsair 4-4-0 saddle tanks with a leading bogie axle, a major innovation in design at the time.

While the GWR slowly took over many other lines, including standard gauge, Gooch came to accept with much disappointment that the end of broad gauge would be inevitable, and began drawing up plans for standard gauge locomotives.

His last broad gauge class designed for the GWR was the Metropolitan Railway 2-4-0 tank engine, with 22 being built between 1862 and 1864. Class members were fitted with condensing apparatus to nullify the discharge of steam in the tunnels of what became the London Underground system.

In total, 407 broad gauge and 98 standard gauge engines were built to Gooch designs, 340 of them in 'his' works at Swindon.

Gooch, a freemason, resigned his post as locomotive superintendent in 1864 to concentrate on

laying undersea telegraph cables, and was appointed chairman of the Telegraph Construction and Maintenance Company and director of the Anglo-American Company. He became a baronet for his work in laying the first transatlantic cable, which he achieved using the *Great Eastern*, the biggest of all the steamships built by none other than the man who gave him his first big break, Brunel.

On 27 July 1866, Gooch sent the first telegraph cable from Newfoundland to Britain. Ironically, he became more famous in his day for his work in telecommunications than in locomotive engineering.

In 1865, he was elected as a Conservative Member of Parliament for Swindon's neighbouring town Cricklade, and represented it for 20 years, although never made a speech in the House of Commons. Also in 1865, when the GWR, along with other railway companies, sunk into severe financial difficulties, its directors persuaded him to return as chairman – with spectacular results.

At the helm of the GWR, it was Gooch who decided that a new carriage works would be built at Swindon, not in Oxford.

In the 1880s, as GWR chairman – a position which Brunel never reached – Gooch was a staunch supporter of the Severn Tunnel project, and first travelled through it by train on 5 September 1885.

Gooch died at his luxurious home at Clewer Park, near Windsor, on 15 October 1889 and he was buried in St Andrew's church in nearby Clewer.

The Times had issued daily bulletins on his health in the days leading up to his death. No other British locomotive engineer would be publicly honoured to that extent.

His name is remembered in Swindon today in Gooch Street near the railway, and the Sir Daniel Arms pub in Fleet Street, near his Railway Village. His brothers John Viret Gooch, Thomas Longridge Gooch and William Frederick Gooch were also railway engineers.

Gooch is remembered as 'the father of Swindon Works'. While his locomotive designs were bettered by his successors, and broad gauge inevitably died, he paved the way for the GWR to grow into one of the most widely respected railway companies anywhere in the world. ■

Lord of the Isles, **built at Swindon in 1851 and exhibited in Chicago in 1893.**

Swindon Works

Murdock, outshopped from Swindon in May 1865, was one of Armstrong's Hawthorn class of 2-4-0s and was built in 1865.
BROAD GAUGE SOCIETY

Steady progress as Swindon expands

After Daniel Gooch resigned as locomotive superintendent in 1864, he was replaced by Joseph Armstrong. He too would leave an indelible mark, both on Swindon and its railway history, despite occupying the role for only 13 years until his sudden death in 1877.

He was a great engineer in his own right, and a highly practical one, yet it is for his sympathetic management of developments at Swindon at an extremely difficult time that he is best remembered.

Armstrong was born at Bewcastle in Cumberland in 1816, the same year as Gooch. An accomplished engineer in his own right, he gained his first railway experience as a driver, right at the birth of railways on the Stockton & Darlington Railway – the world's first public steam-operated line – and on the Liverpool & Manchester Railway.

When the amalgamated standard gauge Shrewsbury & Birmingham, and Shrewsbury & Chester Railways were merged with the GWR in 1854, Armstrong became superintendent of the northern division at Wolverhampton.

A decade later, he replaced Gooch as GWR locomotive superintendent, not only in charge of the locomotive works, but also of the new carriage and wagon department.

Armstrong, a dedicated Wesleyan Methodist and lay preacher, worked tirelessly to ensure that the plans for Swindon's new carriage and wagon works, on which construction began in 1868, were implemented.

Like Gooch before him, he had the well-being of the company's employees at heart, and actively supported all the social facilities and provisions that had been set up to serve them in Swindon.

In 1866 he helped to form the Swindon Water Works Company so that the town could at last have an adequate water supply, which came two years later. Previously houses in the Railway Village had been provided with piped water, but it had been taken out of the canal.

The town's first sewers were laid in 1866, although they merely emptied into a ditch until a sewage works was built in 1872. The GWR opened the Medical Fund Society Hospital, of which Gooch had laid the foundations, and in 1869 swimming baths were

Joseph Armstrong, the second locomotive superintendent of the GWR.

One of Armstrong's Rover class 4-2-2 express passenger locomotives hauled the last through broad gauge train from Paddington to Penzance, the 'Cornishman' pictured prior to departure from London at 10.15am on 20 May 1892. GWR

opened for the use of the workers.

Armstrong became a hugely popular figure in the community as a result of such innovations, and despite the financial morass in which the GWR found itself when he took over, he oversaw a crucial period in which the great works were transformed from a straightforward, predominantly repair facility, to a self-supporting engineering factory, bestowed with a new carriage and wagon works and burgeoning locomotive production.

In six years he doubled the floorspace of the works, and in 1872, the famous Swindon Works' hooter was first sounded. Some said it could be heard six miles away, and at its call the main entrance in Emlyn Square became crowded with hundreds of workers who piled out of their nearby homes.

In the eight years from 1869, when the works was in full production and his death, Armstrong oversaw the building of around 600 locomotives, 2000 carriages and at least 10,000 wagons.

His own designs were simple, and by no means as ground-breaking as those of Gooch, but they were practical and reliable. Around 40 Armstrong engines were still running at the end of WWII.

However, under Armstrong, only 70 more broad gauge engines were built.

The first batch was his Hawthorn class of 26 2-4-0 tender engines with 6ft driving wheels, some of which were later converted to saddle tanks, but they were built by Slaughter, Gruning & Co (later the Avonside Engine Company) in Bristol and were named after famous engineers.

Then there was the Swindon class of 14 0-6-0 goods engines which appeared in 1865-66 and were all sold to the Bristol & Exeter, returning eight years later when the GWR finally absorbed that company in 1874.

The only side tanks built for the GWR broad gauge were the six Sir Watkin class 0-6-0s, which

appeared at the same time, and were at first fitted with condensing gear for use on the Metropolitan Railway. Three were sold to the South Devon Railway in 1872, and all six were rebuilt as saddle tanks.

Armstrong also produced standard gauge 2-4-0 tanks for the Metropolitan Railway, again fitted with condensing gear so they could work underground through to Moorgate Street and Liverpool Street. When the route was electrified, the condensing gear was removed, cabs were added and the type found use on branch lines on the GWR system.

Last, but certainly not least, of all the broad gauge types came the 24 Rover class 4-2-2s, which succeeded the legendary Iron Dukes of Gooch.

Three Iron Dukes, *Great Britain*, *Prometheus* and *Estaffete*, were extensively rebuilt in 1870. They were given new frames and boilers, but kept their original names. The next year, the first of a 'new' series of locomotives built to similar specifications emerged. These not only replaced Iron Dukes as they were withdrawn, but kept their names.

They were called 'renewals', but unlike the aforementioned trio, they were not rebuilt from Iron Dukes, but all new, although, it is said *Rover*, *Swallow* and *Balaklava*, the first three to be outshopped, may have included some parts from their 'predecessors'.

The new locomotives became the Rover class. While closely resembling the Iron Dukes, they differed in having vacuum brakes on both the driving and trailing wheels. By comparison, the Iron Dukes had brakes only on the side of the tender, and none at all on the engine.

The first three were fitted with the original Iron Duke weatherboards that offered little protection for the drivers and firemen. The three that followed in 1873, *Hirondelle*, *Iron Duke* and *Timour*, had iron roofs, which offered much more protection, although they rattled badly. From 1876, all members of the class had wooden cab roofs.

Swindon Works

Rover, the first of the class when it emerged from Swindon Works in August 1871, and one of three fitted in 1888 with bigger boilers, set the mileage record for the class, clocking up a total of 787,174 between 1871 and 1892.

The Rovers mainly saw service on expresses between Paddington and Bristol.

The last to be built was Tornado, outshopped in July 1888, and like sisters Great Western and Prometheus, saw just four years' service before the broad gauge was abandoned and they had to be scrapped.

Gooch did not live to see the end of broad gauge, but his successor had begun preparing for the day. Under Armstrong, Swindon built 112 'convertibles' that could be switched from 7ft 0¼in gauge to 4ft 8½in when the time came.

The first convertibles appeared in late 1878 with 10 Armstrong 0-6-0 saddle tanks. These were one of the most durable of Armstrong's standard gauge designs and the 1076 or Buffalo class were so called after the naming of No 1134. They were built to a basic standard gauge design with double frames so they could be converted to run on broad gauge (50 were, and back converted when 7ft 0¼in gauge ended) the last was withdrawn in 1946.

Also converted were 20 double-framed 388 class or Armstrong Standard Goods 0-6-0s that had previously run as standard gauge engines. A total of 310 examples of the 388 class had been built in several batches between 1866 and 1876.

From then on, the GWR built no more engines exclusively for 7ft 0¼in gauge. As older broad gauge engines were withdrawn they were replaced with 'convertibles'.

The most famous Armstrong locomotive was probably his 7ft single 2-2-2 Queen, which appeared in 1873. It worked all the important standard gauge trains out of Paddington, and frequently saw service on the Royal Train itself.

The news of Armstrong's death at the age of 61, from a heart attack following nervous exhaustion as he was on his way to Matlock in Derbyshire to take hydropathic treatment as part of a three-month rest cure, was met with widespread grief in Swindon, followed by the town's biggest-ever funeral.

A year after Armstrong's death Astill's *Original Swindon Almanac* of 1878 recorded that the loss of the locomotive superintendent "cast a gloom over the entire community".

A crowd of 6000 lined the route of the funeral procession to St Mark's church in the Railway Village where he was buried in the new cemetery. Gooch himself headed the delegation of GWR directors.

Swindon workers clubbed together to buy a lifeboat for the RNLI as a memorial to Armstrong. It was stationed at Cadgwith in Cornwall, a picture-postcard fishing village that has inspired generations of artists. It subsequently became a favourite holiday haunt of many senior GWR officials. ∎

A contemporary colour postcard of a Rover 4-2-2 at speed. Armstrong's Rovers were 'upgrades' or, rather, total rebuilds of the hugely-successful Iron Dukes and continued the evolution of world-beating technology at Swindon.
BROAD GAUGE SOCIETY

A Metro tank fitted with condensing apparatus allowing it to work on the underground. The loads hauled and speeds obtained by this class, designed mainly for London suburban working, was considered remarkable for such small engines.
GWR TRUST COLLECTION

Dean Goods 0-6-0 No 2561, an example of a masterful Swindon-built class that eventually numbered 280 examples and which refused time and time again to give up the ghost, and saw service in World War Two on both sides! GWR TRUST COLLECTION

WILLIAM DEAN

The great
moderniser

Oil painting by F Moore illustrating the last broad gauge train going west on the Great Western Railway, in Sonning Cutting on 20 May 1892. William Dean presided over the end of one era – and the beginni ngs of an even greater one... COURTESY NATIONAL RAILWAY MUSEUM

William Dean, the third locomotive superintendent of the Great Western Railway. GWR

Joseph Armstrong was replaced as locomotive superintendent by his apprentice William Dean. Born in 1840, Dean was the second son of Henry Dean, manager of the Hawes' soap factory in New Cross, London. At 15, Dean became an apprentice under Armstrong at Wolverhampton's Stafford Road Works, and after he finished his indentures in 1863 became his chief assistant. He graduated to a similar position under Armstrong at Swindon in 1868.

At the age of 37, after his superior's death, Dean found himself lumbered with the job of tackling the end of the broad gauge era, and producing a new breed of locomotives, not only for the standard gauge that would finally replace it, but which could be adapted to run on both during the 15 years leading up to the final conversion.

By and large, Dean built basic but highly effective

locomotives, including the 280 0-6-0 freight locomotives that came to be known as the Dean Goods, and which not only gave sterling service throughout the Paddington empire – they have been described as the 'workhorse' of the GWR – but also saw service on the continent in two world wars.

In 1900, in a bid to meet the increasing demand for more powerful engines to work heavy coal trains from South Wales, he introduced another class for which he is well remembered, the Aberdare 2-6-0.

The Aberdares were, in broad terms, a freight version of Dean's Bulldog passenger 4-4-0s. While they were all withdrawn by 1934, some returned to service during WWII, but all had gone by 1949.

His Duke 4-4-0s, introduced in 1895, and his comparable Badminton class, proved very successful on the steep gradients of Cornwall.

The majority of his locomotives, however, were

similar to those of Armstrong, types with a large single driving wheel, such as his 4-2-2 express locomotives, one of which averaged 72mph from Bristol to London in 1904.

The Dean Single or 3001 class was built between 1891 and 1899, the first eight as convertible broad gauge 2-2-2 locomotives, and a further 22 as straightforward standard gauge engines.

Sadly, owing to their long boilers, these engines were unstable, particularly at speed, and despite remedial modifications, including adaptation of the design to a 4-2-2 wheel arrangement to reduce the weight on the front wheels, they soon became overtaken by technological development, and were all scrapped between 1908 and 1915. Nonetheless, No 3065 *Duke of Connaught* made a record-breaking run with the 'Ocean Mail' on 9 May 1904, running from Plymouth to Paddington in 227 mins.

Dean's Duke class 4-4-0 No 3272
***Amyas*, built in August 1896.**
GWR TRUST COLLECTION

However, Dean's Atbara class of 4-4-0s, similar to the Badmintons but with much larger boilers, marked a watershed in GWR locomotive design, ending the company's tradition of single driving wheels for fast express trains, and paving the way for the types which raised the company to dizzy new heights after the end of the Victorian age.

Dean also constructed a series of experimental locomotives, including No 9, which was built in 1881 as a 2-4-2 tank engine that derailed in front of him while on its first test run. The only tank locomotive built by the GWR with single driving wheels, in 1884 it was rebuilt as a 4-2-4 tender locomotive, and six years later it underwent another transformation, into a 2-2-2 which resembled members of Armstrong's Queen class and accordingly was named *Victoria*.

It was during Dean's tenure that 6ft 8½in driving wheels were introduced, becoming a popular feature of GWR design. Also, he gave locomotives increased cylinder sizes, increasing power at a stroke.

He inherited the complicated broad-versus-narrow gauge problem that forced him to build 'convertibles' (standard gauge rolling stock temporarily converted to run on the broad gauge). By 1892 the broad gauge battle was finally lost and the whole network converted to standard gauge (almost overnight).

One of Dean's biggest improvements was his decision to provide cabs for engine drivers. Armstrong had persistently refused to do this because he believed that open footplates prevented drowsiness.

Larger carriages emerged under Dean, whose stock featured the first lavatories and electric lights, heralding a new era of passenger comfort.

Under him, the corridored train, carriage heating and the prototype modern sleeping car emerged from Swindon. Indeed, goods engines apart, Dean is probably best remembered for his work on carriages.

Dean set up the Swindon chemical and materials testing laboratory, in a bid to improve the quality of metal used in locomotive construction. In 1893, he presented a paper to the Institute of Mechanical Engineers entitled *Tensile Tests and Chemical Analysis of Copper Plates from Fireboxes on the Great Western Railway*.

For many years it was standard reading for locomotive designers. Like his predecessors, Dean also made a personal input into Swindon and its community.

He helped found of a branch of the St John Ambulance in the Swindon Works, becoming its president until his retirement. He also became president of the Mechanics' Institute, and in his spare time attained the post of captain and then honorary major with the 2nd Volunteer Battalion of the Duke of Edinburgh's Wiltshire Regiment. He was also a county magistrate.

During the last few years before his retirement in 1902, Dean's health increasingly suffered, his mental faculties were failing, and more and more work was delegated to his assistant, George Jackson Churchward, who took on his day-to-day responsibilities, and perhaps most importantly, was given the freedom to develop his own designs.

Dean died at his retirement home in Terlingham Gardens, Folkestone, three years later.

Of the Dean Goods, only one example survives, No 2516, which is on static display at STEAM – Museum of the Great Western Railway at Swindon.

While no member of the Dean Single class survives, a static replica of No 3041 *The Queen*, built by Madame Tussauds for its Railways and Royalty exhibition at Windsor & Eton Central station, is still on display there. Class sister No 3046 emerged in the early 60s as a Triang 00 gauge model locomotive, reissued by Hornby as a special collectors' item in 2006 both in its *Lord of the Isles'* identity and that of No 7 *Lorna Doone*. ■

Dean single 4-2-2 No 3032 *Agamemnon* as built.
GWR TRUST COLLECTION

Dean No 7 class 4-4-0 No 8 *Gooch*, built in May 1894 and named after the man who built Swindon Works, seen at Westbourne Park in London.
GWR TRUST COLLECTION

Churchward designed and built the first British Pacific at Swindon. *The Great Bear* is seen heading through Swindon with the 'Cheltenham Express.' GWR TRUST COLLECTION

George Jackson Churchward

George Jackson Churchward, whose designs set the scene for Great Western steam in the 20th century. GWR

D ean's successor, George Jackson Churchward, would become much more than the fourth in a line of GWR locomotive superintendents.

In hauling Brunel's railways from the Victorian era into the modern age, he would be hailed by some as the most brilliant of all British locomotive engineers, even though others would follow who, elsewhere in the country, would build better engines.

Churchward's reign marked the end of the GWR epitomised by locomotives with oversize brass domes, stovepipe chimneys, single driving wheels and minimalist cabs.

His designs set the scene for steam in the Paddington and Swindon empire right through into the British Railways' era and later dieselisation. They are the types that most schoolboy trainspotters of the 50s and 60s, or visitors to heritage railways that run GWR locomotives, would recognise instantly, even if they had been modified or adapted by his successors.

Yet Churchward was no creative genius on the lines of the Stephensons or Gooch, who came up with all-new ideas. Churchward did not invent radical new forms of traction in a period where the world was looking to electricity, the petrol engine or the gas turbine as a form of propulsion for railway locomotives.

Instead, he took Swindon design technology and construction methods as employed by Dean and refined the various parts, discarding the bad and honing the good to perfection. Adaptation and refinement, not outright invention, marked his undoubted brilliance.

He made the GWR name a hallmark of excellence, a railway that was the envy of the world, and which others tried to emulate.

It has been said that his designs set the standards that other great British steam engineers of the 20th century followed, in one way or another. What the Brunel and Gooch combination was to the 19th century, so Churchward was – and possibly more – to the 20th.

Churchward was born on 31 January 1857 in Stoke Gabriel near Paignton in Devon, and at school excelled at mathematics.

At 16, he joined the still broad gauge South Devon Railway, working under its locomotive superintendent, but three years later, found himself in the GWR drawing office at Swindon, working his way up to become manager of the carriage works, works' manager and eventually chief assistant to Dean.

Aged 45, he became locomotive, carriage and wagon superintendent, the title being replaced by the more 'modern' chief mechanical engineer in 1916.

Having worked under the ailing Dean, Churchward had time to assess his empire to be and work out how to reshape it to meet the needs of a far more demanding century.

One of the big problems was the multitude of different types of locomotives that he inherited, not only those from the smaller lines that the GWR had absorbed, but types built to different variations within the company itself.

Standardisation would be his keynote, not only of parts that were interchangeable between certain or all classes of engine type, but less than a dozen locomotive classes. The advantages were obvious: easy access to spare parts, less turnaround time in the works, standardised knowledge throughout the workshops and sheds of the system, and a far more efficient company. Boilers, wheels, cylinders, motion and tenders were all henceforth to be built to standard designs.

Influenced somewhat by American developments, Churchward evolved the boiler into four standard types, different sizes to match that of the engine types. Dean's round-topped firebox was replaced by the flat-topped Belpaire type, which had a narrow

sloping grate to burn the coal more efficiently, and larger water spaces to provide more steam at the hottest part of the boiler.

Another big advance in the boiler field was the provision of tapered types to help steam formation. The tapered boiler is the most instantly recognisable feature of Churchward's engines.

He did not rush out to build new batches of locomotives as soon as it had been confirmed that Dean's empire was at long last his.

Instead, he experimented on a massive scale, assessing the strengths and weaknesses of the existing types and trying out modifications wherever possible.

Only then did he reach for the drawing board, harnessing an imagination backed to the hilt with reams of empirical data, and a determination to excel.

Within two years, with his first design, he ensured that the GWR would be immortalised in the history books…

He knew that he could not replace a fleet of 3000 old or non-standard locomotives overnight, but between 1903 and 1911 he turned out nine standard new types, maximising component standardisation.

He remodelled Swindon Works, providing a new one-and-a-half acre boiler and erecting shop, and in 1904, a landmark year for the steam engine, built the first successful locomotive testing plant in Europe.

Carriages were not forgotten. His 70ft main line coaches and other vehicles elevated passenger comfort to new levels.

Churchward retired in 1922. There was bitter irony in his death at the age of 75 on 19 December 1933 when, while walking from his Swindon home to the works (which he still visited frequently) in thick fog, he stepped in front of a main line steam train and was killed. ∎

Above: Churchward heavy freight 2-8-0 No 3802 is today very much a passenger engine, seen here in Llangollen Railway traffic on 21 April 2007, about to haul a brake van special during the line's hugely-successful Steel, Steam & Stars spring steam gala. ROBIN JONES

Above left: The five members of the 1361 class of 0-6-0 tank engines appeared out of Swindon Works in 1910, and were built to operate on lines around Plymouth and Weymouth docks. Their 11ft wheelbase could easily negotiate 66ft radius curves of 2 chains in radius. It has been said that they were a modernised version of the Cornwall Railway's 1391 class. They were designed by Harry Holcroft, assistant to Churchward. All five were replaced by diesels in 1961/2, but No 1363 survives at Didcot Railway Centre, where it is seen on a snowy day in the 1970s. GREAT WESTERN SOCIETY

Swindon's greatest legend

It was on 9 May 1904, on Wellington Bank on the Bristol-Exeter main line, where Gooch had demonstrated that his Swindon-built broad gauge engines were indeed world-beaters, that one of the products of the great works at Swindon was immortalised.

City of Truro

The first steam locomotive to break the 100mph barrier was recorded as having attained 102.3mph while descending Wellington Bank with the 'Ocean Mails Special' from Plymouth to Paddington.

The feat was not acknowledged by the GWR until three years later, even though a report of the event appeared in a newspaper the following day, as a mail van worker on board had conducted some unofficial timings of his own.

Nonetheless, when all was eventually out, the world's attention again focused on the steam engine and its huge potential – and that of Swindon Works.

No 3440 *City of Truro* (later renumbered 3717) was an example of Churchward's first designs, the 20-strong 4-4-0 City class, designed for hauling express passenger trains. Half of these locomotives were rebuilt from Dean's Atbara class engines, the first (No 3405) being converted in September 1902 and the rest following between 1907 and 1909. The other half was built at Swindon in 1903.

At the time, the GWR was engaged in fierce competition with its great rival in the West Country, the London & South Western Railway, to see which could bring ocean mails from Plymouth to London the fastest, and while they had not been given permission to do so, some of the GWR's drivers were determined to show what they and their Swindon-built engines could do.

On the day, it was the job of driver, Moses Clements, to take the train to Paddington, and by the time the train, hauling a load of eight-wheeled postal vans with around 1300 large bags of mail on board – total load weight 148 tons – had reached the South Devon banks, it appeared that he had decided to 'go for it'.

By the time the locomotive was racing down from Whiteball Tunnel on the far side of Exeter, it was going faster than any member of the class had gone before.

On the footplate was timer, Charles Rous-Marten, who at around 10.45am recorded a quarter mile in 8.8 secs while descending Wellington Bank, hence the 102.3mph claim.

Unfortunately, the driver spotted a gang of platelayers standing in their way a quarter of a mile ahead, and had to brake fiercely while they moved aside, which meant that they carried on and into Taunton at just 80mph, ruining the recorder's chance to confirm the speed.

Furthermore, there was no secondary timer on board to confirm the claimed speed, so it was never taken as an official record.

At first Rous-Marten kept quiet about the 102.3mph claim, and when he wrote an article that appeared in *The Railway Magazine* a month later, he merely described the trip as setting "the record of records".

He watered down his account on the instructions of the safety-conscious GWR, which was aware of growing public concern about super-fast trains in the aftermath of the derailment of a night tourist train at Preston during the 'Race to Aberdeen'. And so, only the overall timings for the run were allowed into print.

"It is not desirable at present to publish the actual maximum rate that was reached on this memorable occasion," wrote Rous-Marten. He restricted his account to reporting that the train reached the minimum of 62mph logged on the ascent to Whiteball.

The GWR eventually relented, and in December

Below: *City of Truro* had been preserved for more than a third of a century when British Railways decided to bring it back into revenue-earning traffic in the late fifties. It is pictured at Sutton Scotney on 13 July 1957.
GWR TRUST COLLECTION

1907, *The Railway Magazine* finally published a table of maximum speeds recorded for various classes of locomotive, mentioning 102.3mph without making it obvious that the top speed was attributed to *City of Truro*. At long last, in the April 1908 edition, the identity of the locomotive was revealed – and in the same month, Rous-Marten died of a heart attack.

The 102.3mph claim provoked a fierce 'did it or didn't it' debate that still rages today. Sceptics claim it would have been physically impossible for a 1000hp locomotive such as No 3440 to travel faster than 92mph on that section of line.

However, the milepost timings provided by Rous-Marten are fully consistent with a speed of 100mph or just over.

It was only in 1922 that the GWR finally publicly boasted about the feat of *City of Truro* and laid claim to the record.

An official record of a steam locomotive breaking the 100mph barrier would not be claimed until 30 November 1934, when the London & North Eastern Railway Pacific No 4472 *Flying Scotsman* achieved the feat when travelling between Leeds and King's Cross.

Yet another question remains: even if Rous-Marten's timings were correct, was *City of Truro* really the first steam locomotive in the world to break the 100mph barrier?

Truro's exploit on Wellington Bank came nearly five years after a series of high-speed test runs on the Lancashire & Yorkshire Railway's Liverpool Exchange-Southport line using locomotives from John Aspinall's newly introduced 'High Flyer' 4-4-2 class.

It was reported that on July 15 1899 one such train formed by No 1392 and five coaches, and timed to leave Liverpool Exchange at 2.51pm, was recorded as passing milepost 17 in 12.75 mins.

While this gives a start-to-pass speed of 80mph, given the permanent 20mph restriction at Bank Hall and the 65mph restriction at Waterloo, the suggestion has been made that this train attained 100mph. Sadly, the railway company never published details or timings of this trip: it is only because passing times

City of Truro **hauls a matching Great Western rake of coaches towards Hampton Loade on the Severn Valley Railway on 13 October 1985.** BRIAN SHARPE

Below left: *City of Truro* **is action on the Bodmin & Wenford Railway in September 2004.** BRIAN SHARPE

Below: One of *City of Truro's* **sister engines, No 3433** *City of Bath.* GWR TRUST COLLECTION

In a 'replay' of its famous trip on the West of England main line, *City of Truro* heads past Horse Cove near Dawlish with the 'Ocean Mails 100' special run by Pathfinder Tours, taking No 3440 from Kingswear to Bristol via Wellington Bank. The locomotive was able to return to the main line after retired London banker Alan Moore, principal sponsor of the Bodmin & Wenford Railway, agreed to pay for the overhaul of its boiler. BRIAN SHARPE

Well away from GWR territory, *City of Truro* heads the 'Scarborough Spa Express.' Bound for York in 1988. BRIAN SHARPE

were unofficially noted by local enthusiasts that the 100mph claim is known at all.

The late David Jenkinson, former head of education and research at the National Railway Museum, said: "It may well have been possible for an engine with driving wheels that size to achieve a feat like that on that particular route. You can probably place some credence on it."

In his 1956 volume, *The Lancashire & Yorkshire Railway*, researcher Eric Mason wrote: "It is likely that the event will probably be regarded in the same light as the GWR *City of Truro* run, because it is alleged no proper records were kept, and has in recent years been taken, rightly or wrongly, with a large pinch of salt."

The design of the City class, unlike most other Churchward designs, looked back to the days of Dean

rather than to the future. Gradually withdrawn, all were scrapped between 1927 and 1931.

Sole survivor *City of Truro* was withdrawn in 1931 and bought by the LNER. The locomotive was placed in a new museum at York.

Incidentally, the LNER was to set an all-time world record for steam speed, when A4 Pacific No 4468 *Mallard* achieved 126mph while descending Stoke Bank in Lincolnshire on 3 July 1938.

In 1957, British Railways decided to return the 'preserved' *City of Truro* to running order and the main line. The renumbered 3440, was used for special excursion trains, mainly on the Newbury-Southampton line.

When it was retired again from traffic in 1961, it became part of the National Collection, which had been set up by the British Transport Commission to preserve key British locomotives.

It was restored to running order again to take part in the 150th anniversary celebrations of the GWR in 1985, and afterwards visited several heritage lines.

Following a public appeal, *City of Truro* was resteamed again in 2004 at a cost of £130,000 to mark the centenary of its unofficial record-breaking run, and returned to Wellington Bank to haul a series of main line specials – albeit nowhere near the speed quoted by Rous-Marten.

Opinions will always remain divided about unconfirmed feats such as this. However, the legend has had far more impact than the physical evidence of the claim.

Whether or not the record was genuine, the world at large wanted to believe it at the time.

It showed an eager public that the steam train could travel safely at speeds of more than 100mph, and that Swindon and the GWR were again leading the field. ∎

The Great Bear, Swindon's biggest steam engine, at Old Oak Common.
GWR TRUST COLLECTION

Churchward's biggest

The Great Bear was the one and only Pacific built by the GWR. Not only that, but No 111, outshopped from Swindon Works in February 1908, was the first 4-6-2 in Britain.

It was restricted to the Paddington-Bristol line because of its size and high axle loading, which gave it a route availability of 'Special Red', although on one occasion it was recorded as having run to Wolverhampton.

Historians repeatedly ask, when Churchward was steaming ahead with his groundbreaking 4-6-0s, why he built a Pacific.

The most likely reason was that he was asked by the GWR board to give the company the distinction of building the first British Pacific, as well as the biggest and heaviest engine of the day.

Other authorities believe that a 4-6-2 was a logical extension of his work with the 4-6-0s. Churchward also wanted to prove that his designs were sound when it came to large locomotive boilers.

His aim appeared to be to show it was possible to build a four-cylinder locomotive with 18in diameter cylinders that could be adequately fed by a standard GWR boiler.

A 36-ton breakdown crane set demonstrates its power by lifting *The Great Bear*.
GWR

The Great Bear experienced early problems with clearance on curves and springing of the trailing wheels. Modifications were also made to the superheating of the boiler. However, with Swindon Works diverting his attention to meeting the demands of military needs in WWI, and Churchward's advances in the development of the 4-6-0s, improvements to *The Great Bear* were not considered a priority.

In January 1924, *The Great Bear*, needing heavy repairs to its boiler after just 527,272 miles, was dismantled and the parts used to build one of Collett's Castle class of 4-6-0s.

Churchward who had by then retired, was disappointed. Two years earlier, when hearing that Nigel Gresley was planning to build a Pacific for the Great Northern Railway (later the LNER), he remarked: "What did that young man want to build it for? We could have sold him ours!"

The locomotive kept its number, but was renamed *Viscount Churchill*, and with an increased route availability, remained in service until its withdrawal in 1953. Sadly, it was later scrapped.

However, Gresley went on to create the A4 streamlined Pacifics, including *Mallard*, the world's fastest steam engine, and the A3s, which included *Flying Scotsman*.

Pacific is one of several names given to common wheel arrangements, a practice started in North America, probably by locomotive builders who wanted informal terms for quick reference.

The 4-6-2s were named Pacifics after locomotives supplied for the Missouri Pacific Railroad in 1902 by US manufacturer Baldwin.

Pacific was one of only a few of the names 'exported' to other countries. A 4-4-2 wheel arrangement is known as Atlantic, possibly originating from the use of such locomotives on the 70mph express train of the US Atlantic Coast Line in 1895, and a 2-6-0 was named a mogul after India's Muhammedan empire.

The name prairie was used for 2-6-2s after US manufacturer Brooks built the type in 1900 for use on lines running across the Mid-Western prairies. ■

As Churchward's City class basked in its reputation as the most powerful inside-cylinder passenger engine of Edwardian design, he followed it up with the County, a class of powerful 4-4-0s with outside cylinders and a short wheelbase.

The last 4-4-0s built by the GWR for use on fast passenger services, they were nicknamed 'Churchward's rough riders' because of their movement when being driven at full power.

By this time, Churchward was moving away from 4-4-0s towards 4-6-0s and the GWR's first four-cylinder locomotives.

Already, several other steam locomotive designers had engaged the marine principle of reusing exhaust steam, which still had considerable energy, in a second but lower-pressure set of cylinders.

Churchward imported French-built De Glehn compound engine No 102 *La France* in

1903 to carry out a series of comparative tests.

The locomotive had two high-pressure cylinders between the frames, with pistons linked to the front driving wheels, and two lower-pressure cylinders visible on the outside of the frames and wheels, which acted on the second set of wheels, making a total of four cylinders.

What Churchward discovered was that the smoother riding of the four-cylinder engine gave huge scope for more power (as well as greater comfort for the driver and fireman).

Despite the fact that compound locomotives had won over the hearts of many, including the London & North Western Railway, Churchward was determined to show that simple, as opposed to compound, expansion could at least equal its power.

Three prototype locomotives were built at Swindon in 1902-03; the first was No 100.

It looked totally different from anything that the

Churchward's Edwardian *scene-setters*

GWR had built before, and in retrospect, had a thoroughly 'modern' appearance, although many contemporary observers expressed disdain for it. The style was said to have had an American influence.

No 100 was the prototype for what became the Saint class of 4-6-0s, and later numbered No 2900, was named William Dean in honour of Churchward's predecessor.

A second prototype, No 98, was built with a half-cone boiler as standard, while a third, a 4-6-0 No 171, later named *Albion* and numbered No 2971, was built specifically to compete with the French compound locomotives, and briefly converted to a 4-4-2 for this purpose.

Rather than opt for a compound design, Churchward chose to build No 171 using two-cylinder simple steam expansion.

While the trials between No 171 and the De Glehn engine were taking place, 19 locomotives were

ordered which were similar to the design of No 171.

Thirteen, of what would become the Saint class, were built as 4-4-2s while the remaining six were built as 4-6-0s, while a final verdict on the best wheel arrangement was reached.

Meanwhile, Churchward wanted further tests using the English and French designs, and ordered two more De Glehn compounds, which eventually became No 103 *President* and No 104 *Alliance*.

The Saint class, which eventually numbered 171 locomotives, was considered to be an ideal medium-size express passenger engine, and went on to give superb service, although crews complained of rough riding.

The last examples had been cut up at Swindon by 1954.

Another of the prototype engines ordered by Churchward was built as a 4-4-2 and given the number 40, but was converted to a 4-6-0 in November 1909 because this wheel arrangement,

Above: The sole surviving Star, No 4003 *Lode Star*, at the National Railway Museum in York. NRM

Above left: Saint No 2902 *Lady of the Lake* outside Swindon shed. GREAT WESTERN SOCIETY

introduced to the GWR with the Saints, doubled the adhesion on gradients.

No 40, built in May 1906, became the prototype of the Star class, designed to haul the fastest trains of the day, and for which another 72 locomotives were built. It was named *North Star*, echoing the Stephenson locomotive that had launched Brunel's broad gauge GWR.

Churchward's Star blueprint drew heavily on the experience of constructing the Saints, but incorporated the De Glehn cylinder arrangement with four cylinders for smoother riding at speed, and two sets of valve gear – but with simple rather than compound expansion – into an otherwise standard GWR design.

Bringing together the best features of the British and French engines on trial, Churchward had produced a masterpiece that would remain the basis of the GWR's larger passenger engines until nationalisation.

Design details that became common on Churchward locomotives, included the method of joining the pair of cylinder castings in the middle of the engine, the long travel valves, the tapered boiler and the generous bearing surfaces. These were absorbed from contemporary American practice, and considered to be revolutionary in Britain at the time.

The four-cylinder Swindon 4-6-0 was here to stay.

In 1908, *North Star*, which became No 4000, and No 4003 *Lode Star*, made history when they were fitted with audible signalling equipment in 1908 as part of the pioneering installation of the Automatic Train Control system between Slough and Reading.

Stars built at Swindon Works from 1910 onwards were equipped with the No. 3 superheater, adopted as standard for hundreds of other GWR engines.

The Stars were highly successful in service and ran greater mileages between repairs than the Saints.

However, the Saints were preferred to the Stars when it came to slow heavy pulling, and were said to hold better when worked at full power to cope with overloading.

Overall, the Saints, which cost less to build than the Stars, were considered better all-rounders than the Stars.

If Churchward had not been greatly impressed by the far superior balancing of a four-cylinder engine in the prototype trials, the Stars may never have been built.

However, when it came to smooth running and wear and tear of the tracks, the Stars were way ahead, and so were used for the big, named, trains of the day, therefore claiming true star quality.

The final batch of Stars was turned out in 1922-23. Under Churchward's successor Collett, five Stars were rebuilt as Castles between 1925 and 1929, and parts of the last 10 were used to help build 10 new Castles in 1937-40.

The sole survivor of the class is *Lode Star*, one of the first batch built at Swindon in 1907, withdrawn by British Railways in 1951 with 2,005,898 miles on the clock.

No 4003 *Lode Star* was preserved at the Great Western Museum in Swindon from 1962, but it 1992 it was transferred to the National Railway Museum, where it is a static exhibit in the Great Hall.

A bold plan by the Didcot Railway Centre-based Great Western Society to create a new Saint, No 2999 *Lady of Legend*, by back-converting No 4942 *Maindy Hall* was, in 2007, nearing completion. ■

Churchward Atlantic No 186 pictured at Bristol.
GREAT WESTERN SOCIETY

Star No 4022 *Bulgarian Monarch* hauls the 'North of West Express' past Tram Inn near Hereford on 2 June 1937. GWR TRUST COLLECTION

Churchward's heavy goods 2-8-0s

In 1903, Churchward produced another first for Swindon Works, the GWR and Britain – the country's first 2-8-0 locomotive. His prototype for the 2880 class, No 97, was streets ahead of most contemporary goods engines in use on Britain's railways, and was leading the way for freight, just as the Saints and the Stars were setting new standards for passenger trains.

No 97 (renumbered 2800 in 1906) was fitted with the GWR standard No. 1 boiler (common to the Saints and the Stars) and had 18in cylinders. To allow extra flexibility over the 16ft 10in wheelbase, the tyres on the second and third pair of driving wheels used thinner flanges and the front coupling rods were fitted with spherical joints in order to permit a small amount of side

play. As with most GWR locomotives, superheating was added from 1909.

The designed load for the class was 60 wagons. However, a test train comprising No 2806, a dynamometer car and 54 wagons began trials with the load progressively increased until 100 wagons were hauled. This figure then became the standard load for the 2800 class. During extensive trials, No 2808 hauled a 107-wagon train of 2012 tons from Swindon to Acton in 1906, thereby setting a new haulage record for a British steam locomotive.

The class members were pressed into service hauling long-distance coal traffic, primarily from South Wales to London, but were also involved in transporting coal for the British naval fleet.

Churchward also proposed a mixed-traffic locomotive using the No. 1 boiler, but never got round to building it. It emerged under his successor Collett as the Grange class of 4-6-0s.

Eighty-four examples of the 2800 class were built. Collett slightly upgraded the design and introduced the 2884 class in 1938, with 81 being built.

The 2800 and 2884 classes hauled much of the long-distance heavy freight trains on the GWR and Western Region for six decades.

The first of the original class to be withdrawn was No 2800 in April 1958, with 1,319,831 miles on the clock, while No 3836 was the last in service when withdrawn in November 1965.

Sixteen members of the class have been preserved – Nos 2807, 2818, 2857, 2859, 2861, 2873, 2874, 2885, 3802, 3803, 3814, 3822, 3845, 3850, 3855 and 3862.

The oldest surviving example is No 2807, built in October 1905, and which in 2007 was in the later stages of restoration to running order by its owning group Cotswold Steam Preservation at the Gloucestershire Warwickshire Railway. It is the oldest surviving example of Churchward's standard designs, and was the oldest engine to enter Dai Woodham's legendary scrapyard in Barry, South Glamorgan.

No 2807 spent its first two decades on coal traffic, but in 1924 transferred to Tyseley to work general freight to London.

In 1958, it moved to Newton Abbot and took its turn on Cornish china clay traffic – it was withdrawn from Severn Tunnel Junction in March 1963. Another example built in that year, No 2818, has been cosmetically restored for display inside the National Railway Museum at York.

Between 1910 and 1923, 105 more 2-8-0s – this time tank engines – were built to a Churchward design.

The 4200 class comprised the first 2-8-0 tanks to be used in Britain, Churchward having back-pedalled from his 1906 plan for a 2-8-2 version because it was

feared that the wheelbase might prove too long for certain areas.

The class shared much with the 2800s, except that a No. 4 boiler was used instead of a No. 1.

These tanks were designed primarily for hauling heavy coal traffic from the mines to the ports in South Wales. The prototype was No 4201.

In 1923, the design was modified to increase the cylinder diameter from 18½in to 19in and thereby raised the tractive effort to 33,170lb. The series that followed became the 5205 class and a total of 60 were built between 1923 and 1940.

When coal exports slumped, several of the class became idle with no other work to do, and were placed in storage at Swindon. There, Collett came up with a new design by converting the 4200 design to a 2-8-2 tank engine by adding a bolt-on extension at the rear which included a trailing wheel. This redesign increased the locomotives' capacity to six tons with the water tanks' capacity increased to 2500 gallons.

Altogether, 54 4200s and 5205s were rebuilt as what became known as the 7200 class.

They too were a success, but their biggest problem was the length of the wheelbase and their difficulty in tackling sharp curves: many sidings were out of bounds to them because of yard derailments.

No 7241 was the first to be withdrawn, in November 1962, and the final four in British Railways' traffic lasted until June 1965.

Saved for preservation are Nos 4247, 4248, 4253, 4270 and 4277. No 4248 is on display in an unrestored state at STEAM – Museum of the Great Western Railway, which has been set up inside the locomotive's 1916-built Swindon birthplace.

Of the 7200s, three survive, Nos 7200, 7202 and 7229. ■

GWR 2-8-0 No 2882 passes Dawlish with a down goods working on 27 August 1961. PETER W GRAY

Opposite: Newly-restored GWR 2-8-0 No 3802 hauls an engineer's train towards Glyndyfrdwy on the Llangollen Railway on 3 March 2006. This magnificent preserved former Great Western line offers spectacular scenery throughout the year. GEOFF LEE

Preserved Churchward mogul No 5322 at Didcot Railway Centre in 1985. Only two examples of the class survive. BRIAN SHARPE

Churchward's *mighty moguls*

I n 1911, the first of Churchward's hugely successful 4300 class of 2-6-0s, otherwise known as moguls, emerged from Swindon Works in the form of the prototype No 4301.

The locomotive was fitted with a standard No. 4 boiler and had support struts similar to those fitted to the 2800 2-8-0s.

The class, which totalled 342 members by the time its production line ceased in 1934, showed its worth from the outset with its all-round ability to take on any form of traffic, from branch line goods to main line expresses.

GWR 2-6-0 No 5355 in passenger service at Ross-on-Wye. GWR TRUST COLLECTION

As a side note, the first 10 4300s were the last locomotives to carry the Swindon worksplate beneath the smokebox. Also, this was the first class to be introduced with top feed as standard.

Eleven 4300s saw service in France with the Railway Operating Division of the British Army Royal Engineers during WWI.

Away from Swindon, Robert Stephenson & Co built 35 examples of the class for the GWR in 1921.

Between January and March 1928, 65 of the engines had weight added in the form of a heavy casting mounted on the front bufferbeam to their pony trucks to relieve wear on the leading driver flanges. They were renumbered in the 83XX series, but reverted back to their original numbers when the castings were removed in the mid- to late-40s.

Despite their usefulness, 88 members of the 4300 series and 12 of the 8300s were withdrawn during 1936-39, their wheels and motion being used in the construction of Collett's Grange and Manor class of 4-6-0s.

British Railways withdrew the last three engines of the class in November 1964.

Just two examples have been preserved, No 5322 at Didcot Railway Centre and No 7325 at the Severn Valley Railway. ∎

The first of the class: No 4700 in an official Swindon Works photograph.
GWR

Express freight
no problem!

No 4703 heads a Plymouth-Paddington service on 19 September 1959.
GWR TRUST COLLECTION

The 4700 class of nine 2-8-0s were the final locomotives designed by Churchward, and the most powerful of heavy freight engine designs.

The class was introduced in 1919-21 for fast goods' work, although its members eventually became known as a mixed freight class because of the power available from their massive boilers, and took turns on passenger services including heavy holiday expresses on summer Saturdays.

Owing to axle loading, the class was restricted in route availability. The prototype, No 4700, was built in 1919 with a standard No. 1 boiler, the same used in the 2800 class, but it proved inadequate, and a new design, the No. 7, was introduced in 1921.

The first to be withdrawn was No 4702 in June 1962, while No 4705 achieved the highest recorded mileage at 1,656,564. The final three 4700s were withdrawn in May 1964.

None survived into preservation, but members of the Great Western Society at Didcot Railway Centre have been drawing up plans to build a new one, filling a major gap in British railway heritage. ■

Prairie No 4566 outside Newton Abbot Works on 15 July 1960. This locomotive, now preserved on the Severn Valley Railway, was the last steam locomotive to be overhauled at Newton Abbot. PETER W GRAY

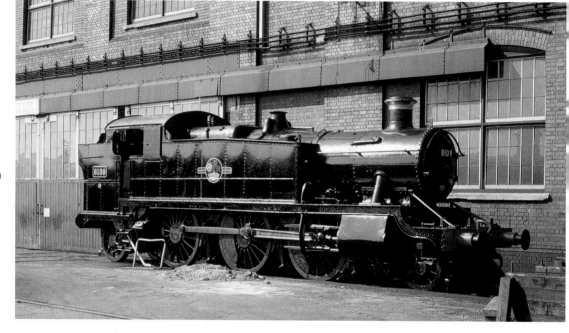

A Collett rebuild of Churchward's prairies with smaller wheels produced the 8100 class, an example of which, No 8109, is seen outside Swindon Works on 24 March 1963. GWR TRUST COLLECTION

GWR 2-6-2T No 4555 leaves Kingswear station with a works train on the Paigngton & Darmouth Steam Railway in June 1992. BRIAN SHARPE

The Great Western prairies

One of the most instantly recognisable and widespread type of GWR locomotive is the prairie tank. Prairies have long been associated with GWR's idyllic country branch lines, as they proved ideal for handling rich and varied types of traffic from the outset. They were the company's general workhorses for six decades.

As you might expect, there were several variations within the GWR 2-6-2Ts, the most basic being the difference between the large and small prairies.

The prototype of the 290 large prairies, No 99 (renumbered 3100, the identity by which the class was known), emerged from the works in 1903 before undergoing two years of trials with the standard No. 2 boiler, and when the design proved sound, a first batch of 39 engines was ordered.

The first modification came in 1906 when 41 members of the class were fitted with the No. 4 boiler and became the 3150 class.

The prototype and Nos 3111-49 were renumbered 5100, and 5111 to 5149, in 1927 and were joined by 50 new engines to become the 5100 class. Members had an axle loading of 17 tons 12 cwt and their bunkers were also enlarged to increase their coal capacity.

The next batch of prairies, the 6100 class (Nos 6100 to 6169) underwent a design change to increase the boiler pressure and tractive effort from 24,300lb to 27,340lb. Forty more 5100 class engines were numbered as the 4100 series. These included the last large prairies to be built, Nos 4140-79.

In 1938, Collett decided to upgrade several members of the 3150 and 5100 classes to further increase their versatility, enabling them to carry out duties such as providing banking assistance. Five 3150s were rebuilt as the 3100 class, using the No. 4

No 4566 leaves Arley with a Severn Valley Railway working on 12 April 1987. BRIAN SHARPE

GWR 2-6-2T No 4136 at Exeter St David's in British Railways days. GWR TRUST COLLECTION

Restored No 5552 recreates the days when the class regularly hauled freight on West Country branch lines. Here it is seen with a restaged china clay working on its Bodmin & Wenford Railway home in September 2005. BRIAN SHARPE

boiler, and 10 of the 5100s became the 8100 class, with the No. 2 boiler.

A smaller version of the large prairie appeared in 1904 after being designed for use on branch lines in Wales and south-west England.

The prototype, No 115, was an overnight success, and while the first batch of 10 engines with 4ft 1½in driving wheels were built on a Swindon Works' lot number, construction took place at Wolverhampton. These were numbered 3101-10, later changed to 4401-10, with No 115 taking its place as No 4000.

The next batch of engines had their driving wheels upgraded to 4ft 7½in to make them more suitable for fast running and to give them a greater range. The

first batch of these, numbered 2161-80, was also built at Wolverhampton, but all those that followed, including the next batch, Nos 2181-90, came out of Swindon Works. In December 1912 they were renumbered 4500-29.

The 4500 series contained two separate classes with Nos 4500-74 with flat-topped tanks, and Nos 4575-99 and 5500-74 with sloping-topped tanks to give increased capacity.

Altogether 175 were built, including those turned out by Collett between 1927 and 1929 with larger tanks.

The first 4000 class small prairie to be withdrawn was No 4402 in December 1949, while three examples soldiered on until September 1955.

In February 1950 No 4531 became the first of 4500 class to be withdrawn. The last one left in British Railways' service was No 4564, which lasted until September 1964.

The first 4575 class locomotive to be withdrawn was No 4586 in April 1956, the final four lasted in service until December 1964.

Ten of the large prairies have been saved for heritage use: Nos 5164, 5193, 5199, 4110, 4115, 4121, 4144, 4150, 4160 and 6106.

Of the small prairies, three examples of the 4500 class and 11 4575s have survived into preservation: Nos 4555, 4561, 4566, 4588, 5521, 5526, 5532, 5538, 5539, 5541, 5542, 5552, 5553 and 5572.

Today, several of these prairies continue to give sterling service on the type of branch lines for which they were built, in the form of heritage railways. ∎

DUKEDOG

Ancient hybrid

Collett again dipped back into the history books when he produced a 'new' design of small tank engines for use on branch lines, the 1400 class of 0-4-2s.

However, his Earl or Dukedog class of 4-4-0s, built for the Cambrian Coast Line between 1936 and 1939, not only looked like it came straight out of the 19th century. It had.

The Dukedogs, a 'renewed' class, were a combination of parts of two classes of 4-4-0, the Dukes and the Bulldogs.

The prototype was Duke No 3265 *Tre Pol and Pen*, withdrawn in December 1929, and subsequently given the frames of Bulldog No 3365 *Charles Grey Mott*.

Twenty-nine more rolled off the production line, with 3ft 2in bogie wheels instead of the 3ft 8in of No 3265.

In 1946, the whole class was renumbered as the 9000-28 series.

It was said that Collett originally named the class Earls in deference to the rich and famous, along with certain GWR directors, who had asked for locomotives to be named after them – and whose pomposity he detested.

It was reported that when a VIP party gathered to view the arrival of first one, and its antiquated outline came into sharp focus, they were horrified.

He was asked to remove the names, some of which transferred to the far more prestigious Castles, but he had had his joke.

With changes in operating conditions after WWII, the hybrid class became increasingly obsolete, the first withdrawals taking place in 1948 and the last in 1960.

No Duke or Bulldog locomotive was preserved, but happily, one Dukedog is still with us today.

No 9017, named *Earl of Berkeley* in preservation, has been based on the Bluebell Railway in Sussex, in hardcore Southern Railway territory, since 1962, and has now been there longer than it ever ran as a Dukedog in GWR service. Indeed, it has become part and parcel of the history of this market-leading heritage line.

Dating from 1938, this example used the frames from Bulldog No 3425 (built in 1906) and the boiler and cab from Duke class No 3258.

It returned to steam in late 2003 following its latest overhaul, and has been booked to revisit GWR metals in the form of the Severn Valley Railway in autumn 2008. ∎

Preserved Dukedog 4-4-0 No 3217 is seen on a rare outing from its Bluebell Railway home on 2 June 1985, in the company of GWR pannier No 3738 and mogul No 5322 at Didcot Railway Centre, for the GW150 celebrations. BRIAN SHARPE

The new erecting shop at Swindon as seen in 1924. GWR

The 100-ton overhead crane in Swindon's A shop carries a 2-8-0 heavy freight tank of the 4200 series. GWR

The GWR's greatest innovator

Charles Benjamin Collett was indeed a great locomotive engineer, but he is not generally regarded as being a genius along the lines of Churchward, who he succeeded in January 1922, as chief mechanical engineer (this had superseded the locomotive superintendent title in 1916).

Nevertheless, under Collett, the GWR was to produce its finest locomotive types, the Castles and Kings, as well as a portfolio of other excellent classes.

By the early 1920s, Churchward's two- and four-cylinder 4-6-0s were leading the British railway field. They were an excellent legacy for Collett.

The son of a journalist, Collett was born on 10 September 1871. His family lived near Paddington station: it may be assumed that the sight and sound of GWR trains during his childhood played a part in shaping his future career.

After studying at London University, he joined marine engine builders Maudslay, Sons and Field of Lambeth.

In May 1893 he moved to the GWR, becoming a junior draughtsman in the Swindon drawing office. Five years later, he had worked his way up to become an assistant to the chief draughtsman.

In June 1900, Collett was appointed technical inspector at Swindon Works and with a few months was promoted to assistant manager.

He finally became works' manager in 1912, and deputy chief mechanical engineer under Churchward in May 1919, a year after receiving the OBE for efforts in producing munitions at Swindon for the WWI battlefields.

Churchward's excellent engines were still ahead of their time, and when it came to finding his successor, an out-and-out locomotive designer was not a priority. Instead, the company looked to a works' manager who could modernise production in the same way that Churchward had revolutionised locomotives.

Unlike Churchward and the GWR locomotive superintendents before him, Collett played little part in the local community, apart from becoming a Swindon magistrate, and by and large remained a private person.

At the Grouping, the GWR inherited many antiquated locomotive types. Operating costs were rising at a time when income was falling, and so there was a need to make the railway more attractive by bringing in even more powerful engines while phasing out several of the pre-Grouping designs and developing more powerful locomotives.

A practical development engineer, Collett took Churchward's revolutionary designs and developed their potential.

Under Collett, Swindon Works modernised and expanded to become the finest locomotive manufacturing and repair base in Britain. He was responsible for a major programme of workshop re-equipment and greatly improved locomotive construction methods.

By 1924, his department employed 45,000 people, with 14,000 of those employed at Swindon Works. From 1926 onwards, he modernised the Swindon testing plant so it could handle the maximum power of larger locomotives.

He introduced a Zeiss optical alignment system for cylinders, frames and motion. It assisted assembly to finer tolerances than previously, and facilitated improvements in wear and performance, leading to a dramatic reduction in maintenance and running costs.

Charles Benjamin Collett. GWR

The nameplate of Collett Castle class 4-6-0 No 7007 *Great Western* as pictured at Oxford in 1962.
GWR TRUST COLLECTION

The General Strike of 1926, combined with a long-running dispute in the Welsh coalfields, crippled the GWR because it relied on coal traffic for a large slice of its income. A short railway strike demonstrated to the public that other forms of transport were available to them.

As a result, reductions in staff at Swindon were inevitable. The GWR as a whole never recovered from the effects of this damaging period, but nonetheless, there was no stopping the continuing rise and development of Swindon Works under Collett.

He also extended the use of the GWR Automatic Train Control system to many of the company's important routes and was a member of the 1927 Pringle Committee which studied the use of such systems in Britain.

Under Collett, the Swindon production line peaked. A total of 103 locomotives were built in 1933, increasing to 150 in 1937. During the same period, the production of coaching stock trebled to 478 while 5340 wagons were made in 1937 compared with 1392 four years earlier.

However, despite his mammoth feats in steam engineering, he was one of the first to advocate the complete dieselisation of the network.

Swindon Borough Council took the unusual step of naming a street after Collett – while he was still in office. Collett Avenue, which was built in 1938, is in Rodbourne Cheney… and runs parallel with Churchward Avenue.

Collett retired from the GWR in 1941, aged 70, and moved to Wimbledon. He died on 5 April 1952 and his small funeral was attended by his successor, Frederick Hawksworth, and Sir William Stanier, his former assistant. ■

Collett masterpieces back at their birthplace: GWR 4-6-0s No 7029 *Clun Castle* and No 6000 *King George V* at Swindon during the GWR 150 celebrations in 1985. BRIAN SHARPE

THE CASTLES

Much, much more
than holding the fort!

Churchward's designs had not advanced since the first superheated Stars emerged in 1910. He was a decade or two ahead of his rivals, but by the time of the Grouping, others were catching up.

So, 1922, when Nigel Gresley's first Great Northern Railway Pacific was built at Doncaster, the GWR board decided that what was needed was a new headline-grabbing big-glamour express engine.

Churchward's Stars were excellent when it came working heavy expresses on the main lines that would take their weight, and in the seven years between their introduction and the outbreak of WWI, they made longer trains possible.

When Collett began his term in office, the company was experiencing a huge upsurge in demand with regards to holiday traffic to the West Country.

Accordingly, the company sunk more money into Paddington-Penzance than any other route – and a locomotive type was needed to become its new flagship.

Collett's team revisited the blueprint of the Stars, enlarging the design by installing a new standard No. 8 boiler with outside steam pipes and a modern cab. The cylinder diameter was increased from 15in to 16in, the grate area was enlarged to 29.4sq ft from 27.07sq ft and several minor mechanical alterations were made.

The design provided a spacious cab, with side windows and comfortable seats for the driver and fireman, and a canopy backing rearwards for improved shelter.

What emerged from Swindon were the most powerful British express engines of their day – the

The 1925 locomotive Exchanges saw No 4079 *Pendennis Castle* in action on East Coast Main Line services. It is seen leaving King's Cross with the 1.30pm to Leeds on 28 April, hauling a rake of London & North Eastern Railway stock. Three decades later, this locomotive found itself in Australia!
GREAT WESTERN SOCIETY COLLECTION

Below: Castle 4-6-0 No 7039 was named *Swindon* after its birthplace.
GWR

Caerphilly Castle, as built, in a Swindon Works official photograph. GWR

GWR 4-6-0 No 5005 *Manorbier Castle* heads the legendary 'Cheltenham Flyer' – once hailed as the world's fastest train – through Cholsey on 19 May 1936.
GWR TRUST COLLECTION

components of the GWR's only Pacific, No 111 *The Great Bear*.

The first Castles appeared with a Star-type tender, and did not receive a high-sided, 4000-gallon version until 1926. The average coal consumption of the Castles was one of the lowest in the country.

Castles hauled the 'Cheltenham Spa Express', which in its day, was the fastest train in the world. On 6 June 1932 No 5006 *Tregenna Castle* set a speed record by covering the 77.3 miles from Swindon to Paddington in 56 mins 47 secs against a schedule that was normally 65 mins. As a result the train became known, unofficially, as the 'Cheltenham Flyer'.

They were also perfectly suited to handling express trains of more than 400 tons over the South Devon banks and the twisting Berks & Hants' route.

The Castles were not the most powerful of GWR designs; that was left to another class, the Kings.

However, the latter's heavier weight barred them from several routes on the GWR network on which the Castles could take their expresses, notably across Brunel's Royal Albert Bridge at Saltash into Cornwall. The Castles were therefore the more useful express passenger engines.

The design of later Castles was slightly modified by Collett's successor Frederick Hawksworth, giving them a larger straight-sided all-welded tender, while other members of the class were fitted with larger superheaters and double blast pipes and chimneys.

The last to be built, No 7037, was named *Swindon* by HRH Princess Elizabeth during her visit to Swindon Works in 1950.

Withdrawal of the Castles began in the 1950s and ended with 1950-built No 7029 *Clun Castle* in December 1965.

This locomotive's finest hour came on 9 May 1964 when, hauling the Plymouth to Bristol leg of a special

Caerphilly Castle on display inside Swindon's STEAM museum in February 2007. ROBIN JONES

excursion to mark the unofficial steam speed record set by *City of Truro* 60 years earlier, it was timed at 96mph, on the same spot, descending Wellington Bank in Somerset.

Clun Castle was bought by enthusiast, photographer and preservation pioneer, Patrick Whitehouse, in 1966 before passing into the ownership of 7029 Clun Castle Ltd and finding a home at Tyseley shed, now Birmingham Railway Museum.

In 1967, *Clun Castle* returned to the main lines to haul special trains, marking the closure of the GWR route, to the company's northern outpost of Birkenhead, as well as specials from King's Cross to Newcastle, and over the Settle to Carlisle line.

Seven other Castles have survived into preservation: Nos 4073 *Caerphilly Castle*, 4079 *Pendennis Castle*, 5029 *Nunney Castle*, 5043 *Earl of Mount Edgcumbe*, 5051 *Earl Bathurst*, 5080 *Defiant* and 7027 *Thornbury Castle*.

Sadly, record-breaker *Tregenna Castle* was not preserved, but its tender survived, and is in storage at the Northampton & Lamport Railway.

Pendennis Castle was sold by owner Sir William McAlpine to Hamersley Iron, one of the largest iron ore producers in Australia, for heritage use and left England in 1977.

After it was left in storage for several years,

Hamersley Iron and its parent company the Rio Tinto Group decided to find it a good home, and in 2000, it was donated to the Great Western Society and repatriated. In 2007, it was being restored to main line running order at Didcot Railway Centre.

After being placed on static display at Paddington and also the Science Museum in Kensington following withdrawal, *Caerphilly Castle* is now preserved at STEAM – Museum of the Great Western Railway. ■

Manorbier Castle, **looking more like a knight than a Castle! Looking at the streamlined Pacifics introduced by rivals the London Midland & Scottish and London & North Eastern railways, the Great Western briefly flirted with applying air-smoothed casings to some of its flagship locomotives in the 1930s, but the trend in the Swindon empire was very short lived!** GWR TRUST COLLECTION

The ultimate GWR design

In the 1950s, when television was still in its infancy and the Sony Playstation had not even been dreamed of, short-trousered schoolboys were not, unlike today's counterparts, spoiled for choice when it came to entertainment.

They either kicked a football around on the nearest piece of open space, went bird nesting, or headed to their nearest railway vantage point with their Ian Allan locospotters' books.

The ultimate ambition of many who chose trainspotting, was to be invited to step onto the footplate of a steam locomotive, with the pinnacle being reached when they were able to 'cab' a GWR King.

This feat was the equivalent today of getting an 'access all areas' backstage pass to meet a pop star. In those days, however, pop stars were few, far between, and normally on the far side of the Atlantic, and so engine drivers were boys' idols.

The class of 30 Kings was the ultimate in GWR power, and was exactly what the company board demanded to see, after its rival the Southern Railway introduced its Lord Nelson class of 4-6-0s in 1926, which bettered the 31,625lb nominal tractive effort of the Castles with 33,510lb.

Collett was told by GWR general manager Sir Felix Pole to reclaim the title of Britain's most powerful steam locomotive, by designing and building a 'Super-Castle' capable of hauling heavier passenger expresses between Paddington and Bristol, the west of England and the Midlands, at average speeds of 60mph.

He came up with what indeed was a larger version of the Castle class, with a tractive effort of 40,290lb – the King class of 4-6-0s.

Many observers wondered why he did not opt for a Pacific, but the shadow cast by *The Great Bear* had not been forgotten at Swindon.

Collett lengthened the firebox and boiler barrel of the Castle design, increasing its diameter by 3in, extended the wheelbase, enlarged the grate and slightly enlarged the cylinders. The King class' 6ft 6in driving wheel diameter was 2½in less than the

Bottom right: Castles and Kings being prepared for duty at Swindon shed on 7 December 1933: from left to right, they are No 5016 *Montgomery Castle*, No 5032 *Usk Castle*, No 6007 *King William III*, No 6021 *King Richard II* and No 6029 *King Stephen*. GWR TRUST COLLECTION

Below: Just as streamlining had been experimented with a view to introducing it on the Castle class, so the GWR gave similar treatment to King 4-6-0 No 6014 *King Henry VII*, but it proved equally as short lived. GWR TRUST COLLECTION

RIGHTS OF WAY ACT
1932
THE GREAT WESTERN RAILWAY COMPANY HEREBY GIVE NOTICE THAT THIS WAY IS NOT DEDICATED TO THE PUBLIC

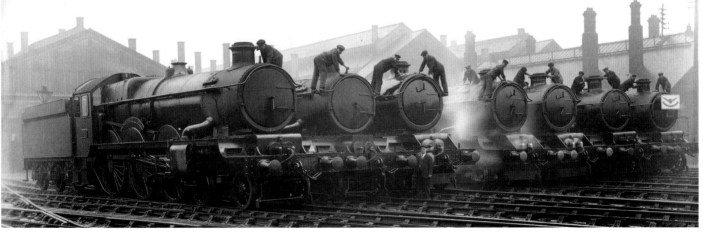

The first of the class and an icon of the post-steam railway preservation movement, No 6000 *King George V* powers through Westbourne Park with a railtour on 1 March 1979. BRIAN SHARPE

'King at Dawlish III': Bridgnorth-based artist John Austin's superb oil painting of King 4-6-0 No 6002 *King William IV* heading across the Dawlish sea wall during a storm surge.

standard for GWR express passenger engines.

A major difference between the appearance of the Kings and other GW locomotives was in the bogie design, which had outside bearings for the leading axle, and inside bearings for trailing to give adequate clearance on curves.

While many of the modifications made to the Castle class were subtle, they marked a major departure from the use of standard Swindon components. Collett decided not to build a new non-Churchward designed locomotive using his predecessor's parts.

As outshopped, the Kings had a boiler pressure of 250lb/sq in, an increase of 25lb over Swindon standards of the day.

Class members were named after kings of England, beginning with the reigning monarch, *King George V*, and working backwards. The final two were later renamed for George V's sons. However, in terms of global transport technology and Swindon products, the Kings were unsurpassed monarchs.

The first, No 6000 *King George V*, emerged from Swindon Works in 1927 and was sent by the publicity-craving GWR on a tour of North America.

There it impressed many at the centenary celebrations of the Baltimore & Ohio Railroad with its modern appearance and excellent performance. The locomotive was presented with a brass bell to mark the great occasion.

It was not only the Americans who were impressed.

London, Midland & Scottish Railway chief mechanical engineer William Stanier – who had been appointed works' manager at Swindon in 1920 – based his Princess Royal class on the Kings, enlarging the boiler and firebox and turning the 4-6-0 wheel arrangement into a 4-6-2.

The Kings allowed the GWR to boast the highest tractive effort available at the time and with its London to Plymouth service, created one of the longest non-stop runs in the country.

However, while the Kings were more than capable of hauling longer and heavier trains, it would be many years before the GWR lengthened the

platforms at many of its major stations in order to accommodate them.

Weighing 22½ tons, the Kings were restricted to the Paddington-Taunton-Plymouth and Paddington-Birmingham-Wolverhampton main lines, which they were given clearance to use only after bridge strengthening had taken place.

Over these lines, they handled prestigious express services such as the 'Cornish Riviera Limited'.

The development of the large four-cylinder 4-6-0s peaked with the Kings, which were renowned for their sure-footedness, tremendous weight-pulling capability, excellent adhesion, safe running and the fact that they were, despite these attributes, light on coal.

During the Locomotive Exchanges of 1948, No 6018 *King Henry VI* did not produce spectacular results on the King's Cross to Leeds route, its supporters claimed that the problem lay with the South Yorkshire coal it used. As a result, Swindon stepped up work on four-row superheaters and improvements to the draughting arrangement.

After these modifications proved successful on No 6001 *King Edward VII*, in July 1953, and double blast pipes and double chimneys were fitted in September 1955 to No 6015 *King Richard III*, the whole class was then modified accordingly.

The Kings were all withdrawn by 1962, replaced by the less powerful Western diesel hydraulics, which they could easily outperform.

Three Kings have been saved for preservation, including *King George V*, which marked the return of steam to the British Rail main line in 1971. It is now a static exhibit inside Swindon's STEAM-Museum of the Great Western Railway.

No 6024 was restored from scrapyard condition and, based at Tyseley Locomotive Works, now hauls regular charters on the main line. Indeed, it has travelled further across the national network than any

other member of the class – visiting destinations as far flung as Penzance, Fishguard, Crewe, Holyhead, Preston, Carlisle, Blackburn, York, Leeds, Doncaster, Norwich, Cambridge, Salisbury, Bournemouth, Weymouth, and GWR's rival London termini of King's Cross and Victoria.

In 1998, it became the first King to be allowed to cross the Tamar Bridge into Cornwall.

In August 2002, *King Edward I* set a new record for steam with the fastest modern-day time for the 52 miles from Plymouth to Exeter, achieved in 58 mins six seconds.

No 6023 *King Edward II* is being rebuilt to main line running order at Didcot Railway Centre, a monumental task, which has included the casting of new rear driving wheels, as the original ones were cut while it languished in Dai Woodham's famous scrapyard at Barry. ∎

On 28 June 1927, *King George V* **came face-to-face with** *North Star,* **the first successful Great Western Railway locomotive.**
GWR TRUST COLLECTION

King No 6027 *King Richard II* **undergoes maintenance inside A Shop at Swindon in early 1932.**
GWR TRUST COLLECTION

The all-purpose *wonder machine*

GWR Hall 4-6-0 No 4953 *Pitchford Hall* takes its first turn on the Vintage Trains summer Sunday 'Shakespeare Express' service from Birmingham to Stratford-upon-Avon, and is seen leaving the great playwright's home town on 3 September 2006.
PAUL STRATFORD

The GWR had, for some years, been looking for a new general all-round locomotive to supersede the Churchward 4300 class of 2-6-0s. On Collett's appointment, he was asked to come up with such an engine. His answer was to look at rebuilding the Saint 4-6-0s, and picked out No 2925 *Saint Martin* as his prototype.

He reduced the driving wheel diameter from 6ft 8½in to 6ft – and created the Halls.

Held as the first true all-purpose mixed-traffic 4-6-0, it eventually became the most numerous GWR tender locomotive, with 259 built to Collett's design.

The Halls proved to be an outstanding success, and were popular with locomotive crews because of their incredible versatility, as they were able to handle traffic right across the board from slow goods to express passenger work.

The Halls went into production in 1928, with a first batch of 80. They were found to be cheap to build, operate, and maintain. Because Collett had evolved an existing mainstream design, little new capital to build them was needed.

Under Collett's successor, Frederick Hawksworth, the design was altered to include modifications to the frames, cylinders and saddle, with larger three-row superheaters fitted at first. These examples became known as Modified Halls, and 71 were built between 1944 and 1950.

The erecting shop at Swindon Works in 1925. GWR TRUST COLLECTION

As a postwar experiment, 11 Halls were converted to oil burning in 1946-47, but had been returned to coal burning by 1950.

After nationalisation, British Railways gave the type a 5MT power classification.

Today's heritage sector has inherited 11 Halls and seven Modified Halls, Nos 4920 *Dumbleton Hall*, 4930 *Hagley Hall*, 4936 *Kinlet Hall*, 4942 *Maindy Hall*, 4953 *Pitchford Hall*, 4979 *Wootton Hall*, 4983

Hall No 5967 *Bickmarsh Hall* seen at Swindon Works in the early 1950s. This locomotive has survived into preservation, but is still an unrestored rusting wreck at the Pontypool & Blaenavon Railway, where its owner was looking to sell it in 2007. JOHN STRETTON COLLECTION

Rood Aston Hall, 5900 *Hinderton Hall*, 5952 *Cogan Hall*, 5967 *Bickmarsh Hall*, 5972 *Olton Hall*, 6960 *Raveningham Hall*, 6984 *Owsden Hall*, 6989 *Wightwick Hall*, 6990 *Witherslack Hall*, 6998 *Burton Agnes Hall*, 7903 *Foremarke Hall* and 7927 *Willington Hall*.

Not all of them have, as of 2007, been restored, nor may ever be. However, two of them, *Maindy Hall* and *Willington Hall*, are forming the basis of projects to build three new locomotives.

Pitchford Hall, owned by Dr John Kennedy and based at Tyseley Locomotive Works, has cost around

£1-million to restore to main line running order from scrapyard condition, perhaps making it the most expensive Hall in history.

The most famous Hall of them all nowadays is No 5972 *Olton Hall*, even though it has been painted bright red in decidedly non-GWR colours for many years.

The locomotive, owned by the West Coast Railway Company, has starred in the Warner Brothers' Harry Potter blockbuster series of films as 'Hogwarts Castle', hauling the 'Hogwarts Express' from Platform 9¾ at King's Cross. ∎

Line-up of GWR 4-6-0 super power at Didcot Railway Centre: from left to right, Hall No 5900 *Hinderton Hall*, King No 6024 *King Edward I* and Modified Hall No 6998 *Burton Agnes Hall*. PAUL CHANCELLOR

A Swindon design – but built by two manufacturers. British Railways' black-liveried No 5637 was built at Swindon Works. It double heads with Brunswick green No 6695, which was constructed at Armstrong Whitworth in Tyneside, on 29 April 2007, during the East Somerset Railway's spring steam gala. No 5637 is based at the Swindon & Cricklade Railway and is on loan-term loan to the East Somerset. No 6695 is part of the Swanage Railway fleet, operating in hardcore Southern Railway territory! Both locomotives were restored from scrapyard condition by volunteers.
ANDREW PM WRIGHT

OLD WINE, NEW BOTTLES

'Carry on as before'

Heavy freight tank engine No 6639 at Swindon in July 1959.
J SUTTON/PAUL CHANCELLOR COLLECTION

At the Grouping of 1923, when the GWR merged with smaller companies that served the South Wales coalfields, the 'Big Four' that came into being inherited a motley collection of 0-6-2 tank engines, which had for several years, been used to transport coal.

While the GWR needed new modern engines for the job, it was decided to stick with this tried-and-tested wheel arrangement.

Collett came up with the 5600 class, which was built with standard GWR parts, such as the No 2 boiler, and 4ft 7½in driving wheels.

The most distinctive feature of the outline of the class is the smokebox overhang that ends at the buffer beam.

The first was outshopped from Swindon in 1924, and the final batch was built by Armstrong Whitworth in Newcastle-upon-Tyne in 1928. Enginemen found that the class ran better in reverse than in forward gear, with the trailing wheel being used as a front bogie.

Two hundred were built, with the first withdrawals made by the Western Region in 1962 and the last in British Railways service, No 6668, running until December 1965.

Nine examples have been preserved, Nos 5619, 5637, 5643, 5668, 6619, 6634, 6686, 6695 and 6697, the last three being built by Armstrong Whitworth. ■

Collett's 'smaller Halls'

Above: Built by British Railways Western Region at Swindon in 1950 to a Great Western design, No 7822 *Foxcote Manor* is today the pride of the Llangollen Raiwlay fleet, and is seen heading a service train through Berwyn station on 8 April 1990. BRIAN SHARPE

Above right: Grange No 6808 *Beenham Grange* heads Castle No 4095 *Harlech Castle* on a heavy passenger working on 13 September 1958.
6880 BETTON GRANGE LTD

Left: Severn Valley Railway-based No 7802 *Bradley Manor* leaves Exeter St. David's in May 1996. This locomotive regularly ran on the main line until 2007. BRIAN SHARPE

Right: Grange No 6817 *Gwendwr Grange* pictured on 7 February 1960. 6880 BETTON GRANGE LTD

As far back as 1901, Churchward had pencilled in a general-purpose class of 4-6-0s with 5ft 8in driving wheels. More than two decades of pressure from the GWR's running department to develop such a type, to replace the 2-6-0s, somewhat died down with the emergence of the Halls.

In 1936, Collett took the Hall design one stage further, producing a smaller version, with 5ft 8in driving wheels, using the wheels and motion from withdrawn 4300s, and raising the platform over the cylinders. Because it was smaller, the 6880 class – which came to be known as the Grange class – had many of the advantages of the Hall class, along with a wider route availability, and proved equally as successful and popular. Eighty Granges – power

classification 5MT – were built up to 1939, with
wheelsets for the first batch coming from withdrawn
4300s. The building programme did not recommence
after WWII.

The first Grange to be withdrawn was No 6801
Aylburton Grange, which was condemned from
Penzance in October 1960. Four of the class,
Nos 6847 *Tidmarsh Grange*, 6848 *Toddington Grange*,
6849 *Walton Grange* and 6872 *Crawley Grange*, lasted
until the end of Western Region steam in December
1965.

None of the class has been preserved, but, what
would have been the next in line to be built at
Swindon, No 6880 *Betton Grange*, is being
constructed by a team of restorationists at the

Llangollen Railway, mainly using standard parts from
scrap GWR locomotives.

Collett was so impressed with the Granges that he
ordered a lighter version – the 7800 Manor class of
4-6-0s – to be built, using a new No. 14 lightweight
boiler and again, reconditioned parts from moguls in
the first batch of 20.

Thirty Manors were built between 1930 and 1950,
the last 10 being all new. Their power classification
was also 5MT.

In the Western Region, the sometimes questionable
steaming, and persistent under-performance of the
Manors was improved through modifications to the
blast pipe and firebars in 1952. Experiments with the
smokebox on No 7818 *Granville Manor* also led to
improved steaming. Modifications included reducing
the blast pipe jumper ring and nozzle diameter from
$5\frac{1}{8}$in to $4\frac{5}{8}$in, which increased the steam rate from
10,000lb/hr to 20,400 lb/hr.

Nearly a third of the Manor class was saved for
preservation: Nos 7802 *Bradley Manor*, 7808 *Cookham
Manor*, 7812 *Erlestoke Manor*, 7819 *Hinton Manor*, 7820
Dinmore Manor, 7821 *Ditcheat Manor*, 7822 *Foxcote
Manor*, 7827 *Lydham Manor* and 7828 *Odney Manor*.

Bradley Manor, one of the first batch to be built at
Swindon, and reputedly constructed from parts of
No 4321, returned to steam in 1993. It has performed
on the main line in recent years and, along with
Hinton Manor and *Erlestoke Manor*, is based on the
Severn Valley Railway. In 2003, it featured on a Royal
Mail 42p stamp as part of a series of six, depicting
classic steam locomotives, and in 2005 it featured in
the Walt Disney big-screen version of CS Lewis' *The
Chronicles of Narnia: The Lion, the Witch and the
Wardrobe*. ■

Collett 0-6-0 No 3205 departs Buckfastleigh in a blaze of patriotic glory. The occasion was a special 'royal train' staged on 2 July 2002 to mark the Golden Jubilee of HM The Queen. Three of the chocolate-and-cream-liveried Great Western Railway coaches in the rake had seen genuine royal service in the past. ROBIN JONES

2251 CLASS

Collett's all-weather workhorse

The sole survivor of a class which once comprised 120 locomotives, Collett 0-6-0 No 3205, a hugely-popular heritage era performer, awaits its next duty in Buckfastleigh yard on the South Devon Railway. ROBIN JONES

Collett's 2251 class of 120 0-6-0 tender engines was built to supersede the Armstrong and Dean goods locomotives in use on routes in mid-Wales. They mainly worked short-haul main line trains and branch passenger services, with the main design feature being a Standard No. 10 boiler and 5ft 2in wheels.

Six of the class, Nos 2281-86, were built with tenders from the Aberdare class that they had replaced.

Twenty class members built in 1940 had the side windows removed from their design, owing to wartime safety fears.

The first member of the class to be withdrawn was No 2258 in December 1958. The last of the class in British Railways' service was No 2210, which lasted until June 1965. The only example to be preserved is No 3205, which made preservation history in 1970 when it hauled the first public train on the Severn Valley Railway, from Bridgnorth to Hampton Loade in Shropshire. ■

Push and pull

Not only did Collett 'improve' recent designs of locomotives to turn them into Swindon world-beaters, but he also delved into the past.

In the early 1930s, he decided to update Armstrong's Wolverhampton-built 517 class, which first saw service in 1879, with several members still in traffic.

The class of 75, built between 1932 and 1936 was first numbered 4800-74, and fitted with auto gear for working auto trains, with the driver able to control the train from a cab at the far end of the carriage while his fireman remained on his own on the footplate.

A later batch of 20 was not auto-fitted, and became the 5800 class.

When members of the 2800 class of 2-8-0s were converted to oil burning as part of an experiment, they were renumbered in the 4800 series, and Collett's original class bearing this number became 1400, with the members renumbered accordingly.

These delightful little tank engines were a typical feature of the GWR's far-flung rural outposts.

However, as unprofitable branch lines were closed by the Western Region years before Beeching, the 0-4-2Ts became redundant. Others were replaced by diesel railcars.

The first withdrawals took place in 1956, and by spring 1961, the 5800 class had gone, none to survive.

The last four 1400s were taken out of traffic in November 1964. Thankfully, four members of the class have been preserved: Nos 1420, 1442, 1450 and 1466. Only No 1442 has never run in preservation, being the centrepiece of the Tiverton Museum in Devon. Previously, it operated services on the GWR branch from Tiverton Junction to Tiverton, and was famous locally as the 'Tivvy Bumper'. ■

Swindon's greatest
steam shunters

Great Western Railway pannier tank No 7714 arrives at Bewdley on the Severn Valley Railway with a demonstration freight train. ROBIN JONES

One type of locomotive that will be forever associated with the GWR is the humble pannier tank. Humble? In its various guises and incarnations, under Collett it became the most numerous GWR class, handling everything from dockyard shunting to branch passenger trains.

The GWR's love affair with the pannier – so called because of the way the water tanks are carried either side of the boiler, like panniers on a donkey, began in the 19th century.

As the Paddington empire grew as more and more smaller railways were absorbed into it, a motley collection of all types of locomotive was amassed.

From the days of mixed gauge, the GWR built many classes and sizes of saddle tank, both at Swindon and Wolverhampton. They included the 1016s, 1076 Buffalo class, 1134s, 1813s, 1854s, 1901s, 2021s and 2721s.

When Belpaire fireboxes were added to the GWR 0-6-0 tank engines of the time, the saddle tanks were often found to be too complicated to fabricate. Side tanks appeared not to be in fashion with the GWR of the day, and when the opportunity arose, many of these saddle tanks dating from 1870-1905 were converted to pannier tanks in the years leading up to WWI. Many of them were given the added luxury of enclosed cabs in the process.

Churchward seemed happy for this process to continue, but in Collett's day, it became clear that these locomotives, many from the days of outside frames, had become half a century old and needed to be supplemented, or in most cases, replaced.

Using the 2721 class, which dated from 1897, as a template, he designed a new type of pannier tank as the standard GWR shunter, and in 1929 the first examples rolled off the production line. The 5700 series, of which 863 examples were built, is the second most-produced British class of steam locomotive.

Unlike the 2721s, the 5700s had Belpaire fireboxes, closed cabs and large extended bunkers.

Three quarters of the class members were built at Swindon Works, with the rest by private builders; Armstrong Whitworth, Bagnall, Beyer Peacock, Kerr Stuart, North British and the Yorkshire Engine Co.

Pannier No 9628 takes the 3.17pm service from Frome to Yatton into Shepton Mallet on 24 February 1962. Part of this cross-country route, the Cheddar Valley line, is now the East Somerset Railway. GWR TRUST COLLECTION

Pannier No 6400 heads the 3.25pm service from Exeter at Cadeleigh station on the Exe Valley Line on 16 March 1963. This station is now restored as the headquarters of the Devon Railway Centre, which runs a two-foot gauge line along the old trackbed. PETER W GRAY

There were so many of the type built that they had to be numbered in nine different series: 3600-99, 3700-99, 4600-99, 5700-99, 6700-79, 7700-99, 8700-99, 9600-82, and 9701-99.

One tiny subclass, numbered 9700-10, was fitted with condensing gear for working meat traffic over the Metropolitan and Hammersmith & City Lines to Smithfield market, replacing earlier 'Metro' and 633 class locomotives.

Another 13 received spark-arresting chimneys for working in military depots where munitions were stored.

With diesel shunters taking over its duties, the 5700 class was withdrawn between 1957 and 1965. Thirteen members were sold to London Transport for use on the Underground, where they operated until 1971, while others found their way into National Coal Board ownership and continued to operate for several years after the end of British Rail steam in August 1968.

The last 5700 in industrial service was No 7754 at Mountain Ash colliery, where it was working well into the 1970s and could still be seen on shed in

The myriad of lines in the Dean forest and Along the Wye Valley relied heavily on pannier tanks for both freight and passenger workings. ROBIN JONES

1980. It is now part of the Llangollen Railway fleet.

Sixteen members of the 5700 class have entered the heritage sector: Nos 3650, 3738, 4612, 5764, 5775, 5786, 7714, 7715, 7752, 7754, 7760, 9600, 9629, 9642, 9681 and 9682.

The 5400 class was similar to the 5700, but with smaller wheels and boiler and designed for push-pull passenger work. Twenty-five members were built between 1931 and 1935 to Collett's design after a prototype was built by transforming 2021 class No 2080.

Although members of the 5400 class were successful, Colett decided that smaller driving wheels would assist in working the hilly South Wales' valleys and therefore designed a new class, the 6400s, for auto-working.

Similar to both these types was the 7400 class, which wasn't fitted with auto-train apparatus and worked in the Welsh valleys on light goods and local passenger services.

The last two 5400s were withdrawn in October 1963, while the final 6400s soldiered on until 1964. The last of the 7400 class were withdrawn in 1965.

Out of the three classes, only three locomotives

survived into preservation, all 6400s: Nos 6412, 6430 and 6435.

The six members of the 1366 class of pannier tank were built in 1934 for dock working, and at first worked taking the 'Channel Islands Boat Express' along the Weymouth harbour branch, and some, including No 1369, the only one to be preserved, were sent to Wadebridge to replace the antiquated three Beattie London & South Western Railway well tanks on the Wenford goods' branch. Others became shunting engines for Swindon Works. The last ones were withdrawn in 1964.

The pannier story did not end with Collett. In 1946, his successor, Frederick Hawksworth, began the building of a further 210, with production lasting up to 1956.

Rather than being based on the 5700s, they were a tank engine version of Collett's 2251 class 0-6-0 tender engine and were the heaviest of the pannier tanks. The first 10 of the class, numbered 9400, were built at Swindon.

Mainly used for heavy shunting and local freight and passenger duties, Nos 8400 to 8406 were moved by British Railways to Bromsgrove to give banking assistance on the notorious Lickey Incline in twos and threes.

Because of dieselisation, the class had a much shorter working life, the last being withdrawn in June 1965.

Two examples are preserved, No 9400 which is on static display at Swindon's STEAM Museum of the Great Western Railway and No 9466, which was built by Robert Stephenson & Hawthorns.

In 1949, Hawksworth introduced an unusual class of 10 heavy shunting panniers, the 1500 class. It broke with GWR pannier design with its outside cylinders, Walschaerts' valve gear and lack of running platform. In addition, most of the separate parts were welded instead of riveted together.

The 12ft 10in wheelbase allowed class members to tackle curves of 115ft radius and they were used in the Newport area and at Old Oak Common as shunting carriages. They were all withdrawn between 1959 and 1963. One survives, No 1501, which has been restored for use on the Severn Valley Railway following its purchase from the NCB's Coventry Colliery mineral branch and sidings at Keresley, where it had worked since withdrawal in 1961.

Finally, under Hawksworth there was the 1600 class, of which 70 members were built at Swindon between 1949 and 1955, to a decidedly GWR style, despite nationalisation.

Not only that, but it was a direct descendant of the 1901-introduced 2021 class, with 4ft 1½in driving wheels.

Withdrawals began with No 1600 in March 1959 and ended with No 1628 in September 1966.

One member survived into preservation, No 1638, which is based on the Kent & East Sussex Railway, well away from GWR territory. ■

No 1501, the sole survivor of the last class of Swindon-design pannier tanks to be built, is now based at the Severn Valley Railway. It is seen in action during a photographic charter at Allied Wire & Steel's Tremorfa Works in Cardiff on 30 July 1999. ROBIN JONES

Great Western pannier No 7754 continued in active service after the end of steam on British Railways in 1968, because it had been sold to the National Coal Board for use on colliery lines. Having been temporarily returned to its NCB livery, No 7754, now based on the Llangollen Railway, is seen on display at the National Railway Museum's Railfest 2004 event at York, which marked the 200th anniversary of the first public run of Richard Trevithick's pioneering steam locomotive.

Hawksworth pannier No 9422 at Swindon Works. GWR TRUST COLLECTION

A rival's engines
built in the works!

William Stanier never rose to the top job at the Great Western Railway, but installed at the rival London Midland & Scottish Railway, he still managed to have one of his greatest designs, his 8F 2-8-0, built there, after Swindon works was ordered to turn out a batch for the war effort. The sole surviving Swindon-built example, No 48431, is seen at Haworth on the Keighley & Worth Valley Railway on 29 July 1986. FRED KERR

Swindon Works made a significant contribution to the war effort in WWI turning out munitions at the rate of 2500 shells a week, while also building naval guns and ambulance trains for use both at home and overseas.

With the workforce already weakened by enlistment, Swindon found itself struggling to cope, not only with running a railway, which in those years was more vital than ever to serving the needs of the country, but also producing equipment for the war effort.

Collett, then works' manager, became increasingly unhappy about the situation, and when WWII broke out, was less than enthusiastic about Swindon taking on military work again.

However, it could not be avoided, for in 1939, Swindon Works, thanks to him, had some of the most modern and sophisticated production lines in the country. Again, the works' highly skilled workforce would be pushed to its limits, and after hostilities ended in 1945, would have to pick up the pieces and rebuild the hub of a railway empire once again.

It goes without saying that much of the wartime activities in the works were carried out under a shroud of secrecy, and because records were locked away, and many staff members were on a need-to-know basis only, much of what went on still remains a mystery.

Most of the munitions work was done between 1941 and 1943, until the USA entered the war and brought in their own in huge quantities.

Nonetheless, more than 60,000 mortar and aircraft bombs were produced. Enterprising as ever, Swindon workers also designed bombs, including the heavy 4000lb sort, which were used in a raid on Essen.

In the aftermath of the Battle of Britain, Swindon also produced aircraft components including more than 170,000 parts for Hurricane fighters.

Gun components were also turned out en masse, the largest being mountings for a hyper-velocity gun used on the Kent coastline for firing at German positions in France.

Components for tanks and armoured cars were turned out by the GWR staff, while the carriage works built powered landing craft and Bailey bridges for the planned invasion of occupied Europe.

Searchlights, radar equipment, and barrage balloon fittings also emerged from Swindon Works as part of the defence of the realm. A full-size model of a midget submarine was built in the works, resulting in orders for 50 superstructures of the real thing.

Part of 24 Shop was given over to Short Brothers for the building of Spitfire aircraft, and was effectively split off from the GWR.

Staff worked long hours, and many of the most skilled GWR workers were loaned out to help set up other factories for the war effort. The works' famous trip holiday for workers was cancelled in 1940, but from September that year, as a concession, staff were allowed to smoke in the workplace, but when doing overtime only. Despite wartime shortages, employees were still allowed to buy coal at a discounted rate.

Diverting such colossal resources to the war effort meant that the railway side was neglected somewhat, with new-building of locomotives almost halved while the number awaiting repairs soared. The problems were exacerbated by

Above: Bombs away! Eight 250lb bombs are loaded at a time on to wagons in A Shop in January 1941 following the placing of an order by the ministry of Aircraft Production.
ROBIN JONES COLLECTION

Below: Milling sprockets for Matilda tanks inside the works. GWR

Below right: A 'Pom Pom' anti-aircraft gun taking shape at Swindon. GWR

staff shortages, which meant that locomotives were not being properly maintained throughout the system.

After the Battle of Britain, several Castles were renamed after British aircraft as a morale booster and fundraising initiative, beginning with No 5071 *Clifford Castle*, which became *Spitfire*.

The works also turned out locomotives for the War Department as well as producing its own engines. Engines were needed for use overseas, especially on routes that linked Russia with Iran.

One locomotive type was singled out for mass production as a general-purpose go-anywhere locomotive, the London, Midland & Scottish Railway Stanier 8F 2-8-0, which had first appeared in 1934. In addition to the 331 that were built by the LMS between then and 1946, Whitehall ordered a further 521 to be built for the war effort, by other 'Big Four' companies if necessary.

A total of 228 of these 8Fs were shipped abroad, many never to return: there are examples still in Turkey and Iraq today.

Orders for 90 of these engines were placed with Swindon in 1942, but because production was limited by the availability of raw materials, just 27 were built in 1943, another 36 in 1944, and 17 in the final months of the war, only 80 being built. They were numbered 8400-8479.

Yes, Swindon Works' staff had to produce engines from one of their closest rivals, but were happy in the knowledge that they had been designed by a former Swindon diehard, William Stanier.

Born on 27 May 1876 in Swindon where his father worked for the GWR, Stanier was educated at Swindon High School. He too joined the company, and after working as a draughtsman from 1897-1900, was promoted to inspector of materials. Four years later, Churchward made him assistant to the divisional locomotive superintendent in London.

Stanier was back in Swindon in 1912 as assistant works' manager, and in 1920 became works' manager. In 1932, he took up an offer to become chief mechanical engineer of the London, Midland & Scottish Railway, taking many Swindon ideas and much Swindon experience with him as he set about producing some of that company's, and Britain's

greatest locomotives, including the Princess Coronation Pacifics.

In addition to the Stanier 8Fs, 33 engines of the GWR 2800 design were also ordered from Swindon for the war effort.

On the railways, it was also a case of 'make do and mend' while obsolete locomotives that had been stored for years or waiting the cutter's torch were brought back into service. The most notable example was the Dean Goods class, 100 members of which were reconditioned for service overseas. They were turned out in War Department black livery, and several were fitted with pannier tanks and condensing equipment.

Seventy-nine were marooned in France after Dunkirk: some of them continued to work on that country's railways during the Nazi occupation.

Some Dean Goods members saw service in Italy, Tunisia and as far afield as China.

Other 'ancient' types were pressed back into GWR service to make up numbers: they included Bulldog 4-4-0s and Aberdare 2-6-0s.

Wartime austerity also dictated cutbacks in raw materials for the railway, including locomotive paint. In April 1942, divisional superintendents were told that Kings and Castles apart, all engines must be reliveried in black, without lining, when they required painting after building or repairs.

The question has been asked – did the Luftwaffe leave Swindon Works alone for the day when the Nazis would conquer Britain?

While 104 bombs were dropped on the Swindon area, killing 48 and injuring 105, and destroying more than 50 houses, during the entire conflict it appeared that the works itself was never seriously targeted, despite its massive importance to Britain's war effort.

The Swindon Works' hooter became the main air raid warning siren for the town, while shelters were provided throughout the factory.

At 6.40am on 27 July 1942, one Heinkel He III bomber dropped five bombs on the northern side of the works, badly damaging the roofs and windows of the running shed and 24 Shop, where munitions work was taking place. A works' gasholder was set ablaze after being machine-gunned. Two GWR staff were injured, in what was the most serious direct raid on the works itself.

On 17 August 1942, a single German bomber dropped bombs close to the works, hitting houses in two nearby streets and killing 24 people. On 29 August that year, a bomb was dropped from 38,000ft killing eight people and damaging more than 300 houses, but yet again, the works was not hit.

Of the Swindon-built Stanier 8Fs, just one, No 8431, survives, and is based on the Keighley & Worth Valley Railway. Built in 1944, it worked on the GWR at Gloucester until 1947, and was then transferred to the LMS.

Numbered 48431, it returned to the Western Region in 1955, and was shedded at Bristol, Old Oak Common and Bath Green Park, from where it was withdrawn in 1964. Restored from scrapyard condition, it entered passenger service on the heritage railway in December 1976. In 2007, it was out of traffic awaiting overhaul. ∎

The sole surviving Dean Goods 0-6-0, No 2516, on static display inside the STEAM museum at Swindon. By then antiquated, scores were pressed into wartime service and many ended up being lost in Nazi-occupied France. STEAM

Hawksworth County 4-6-0 No 1006 *County of Cornwall* at Plymouth's Laira depot in 1962. GWR TRUST COLLECTION

Designer of the Counties

Frederick Hawksworth, the last chief mechanical engineer of the Great Western Railway.

The last GWR chief mechanical engineer, Frederick W Hawksworth, was the only one to be born in Swindon, on 10 February 1884. His father worked in the GWR Swindon drawing office, and he followed in his footsteps by joining the company on 1 August 1898 at the age of 15, as a works' apprentice.

He attended Swindon Technical Institute and won the Gooch Prize for machine drawing.

In 1905 he was appointed to the post of draughtsman, and joined his father in the drawing office. He went on to attain a first-class honours degree in machine design at the Royal College of Science. It was not until 1925 that he became chief draughtsman, and in 1932 became Collett's principal assistant.

When Collett retired in 1941, Hawksworth was chosen as his successor, at the age of 57. Promotion through the GWR ranks during the 20th century was indeed slow. Hawksworth was indeed the right man to restore the GWR to its glory days, but during the years of wartime austerity, the turnover of much of Swindon Works to the military effort and its bleak aftermath would do him no favours.

His hands were tied, and because of the times in which they were conceived, several of his ideas stayed on the drawing board – including one for a second GWR Pacific, which could well have been the most powerful 4-6-2 ever to run in Britain.

Circumstances restricted Hawksworth to improving existing locomotives, producing, as we have seen, the Modified Hall.

The handful of his own designs included new types of pannier tank, and, most prominently, the County class. It was clear that there was a need to change the design criteria that Swindon had maintained largely unaltered since 1902.

For his County class, Hawksworth drew on several concepts that he had devised for his abortive Pacific project in order to produce the final GWR 4-6-0s, ending a line of locomotive development that had begun with Churchward's Saints 42 years earlier.

As already stated, during the war, Swindon Works turned out locomotives to 'outside' designs, including 80 examples of the LMS railway's Stanier 8F.

Hawksworth based his County or 1000 class boiler on that of the 8F, having had the chance to study its design in detail.

He had originally intended the new class to be a larger and more powerful version of the Hall, with four-row superheaters.

However, a new type and larger-capacity boiler than the excellent No. 1 fitted to the Halls, the No 15, was instead devised. The design also included other fresh developments for the GWR including 6ft 3in driving wheels and 280lb/sq in boiler pressure and a continuous splasher over the driving wheels.

By the spring of 1943 the design was ready. It featured a two-cylinder layout, chosen for its low initial cost, ease of maintenance and economy of operation under normal running conditions. The chassis was virtually identical to that of the Modified Hall, which had first appeared in March 1944.

The 30 members of the class, which took their names from the Churchward County 4-4-0s, were given a power classification of 6MT.

The public had to wait until after VE Day to view Hawksworth's first completely new design for an express passenger locomotive, when in August 1945 the first County class No 1000 *County of Middlesex*, emerged from Swindon.

Suffering from early problems and often used for traffic for which they were not entirely suitable, they earned a reputation for being steam shy and uncomfortable to ride behind.

In 1956, the boiler pressure was reduced to 250lb/sq in following earlier tests with No 1026 *County of Salop* in 1952 because of fears concerning hammer blow damage to tracks. The class members been banned by the LMS from the Yate to Standish Junction route, preventing their use on the heavy Wolverhampton to Penzance trains north of Bristol.

Also, a modified chimney and blast pipe was fitted to all members of the class between then and 1959.

Overall, despite complaints from enginemen in their earlier years, the Counties proved themselves capable of outstanding effort, often outperforming designs that were nominally more powerful. Given good coal, careful handling and a diagram that did

not demand constant high steaming rates, a well-maintained County was capable of extremely good work.

The class thrived on the South Devon banks and other notorious gradients in Cornwall because of the traction effort it could produce at high speed.

As with other classes, dieselisation sounded the death knell. In 1962, nine were withdrawn with 13 more going in 1963 with the remaining eight going in 1964. None survived the cutter's torch, being effectively declared redundant in the early 1960s as their work was taken over by diesel hydraulics.

Plans by the Great Western Society to recreate the class by building a replica of No 1014 *County of Glamorgan* have got off to a flying start at Didcot Railway Centre, with the driving wheels being cast in spring 2007.

Hawksworth stepped down as chief mechanical engineer at nationalisation in 1948, ending a line of engineers that had begun with Daniel Gooch.

He continued working in locomotive design with British Railways until he retired a year later. He died in 1976. ∎

No 1016 *County of Hants* hauls the 'Cornishman' through Plympton on 15 July. RC RILEY/GWS

Below left: County No 1009 *County of Carmarthen* heads through Mersham with the 10.10am Bristol Temple Meads to Weymouth direct service on 13 April 1960. GWR TRUST COLLECTION

Below right: The first of Hawksworth's greatest class, the County 4-6-0s, was No 1000 *County of Middlesex*, seen in an official Swindon Works photograph. BRITISH RAILWAYS

Swindon-built BR Standard 4MT 4-6-0 No 75014 *Braveheart* climbs past Goodrington Sands on the Paignton & Dartmouth Steam Railway, the former GWR Kingswear branch, on 3 August 2003. None of the Standard 4s were named prior to preservation. MARK WILKINS/DART VALLEY RAILWAY

Life after the *Great Western Railway*

Despite opposition from the GWR, nationalisation of the railway network by Clement Attlee's Labour government took pace on 1 January 1948.

British Railways came into being as the commercial name of the Railway Executive of the British Transport Commission, which in turn took over the 'Big Four'.

The new system was split geographically into six regions – Eastern, North Eastern, London Midland, Scottish, Southern – and Western. The Paddington/Swindon empire remained intact, albeit under a different name.

Just as the GWR had been forced to cope with the 1923 Grouping after acquiring odd assortments of locomotive and stock from absorbed companies, so the new national railway company inherited the widest selection possible – 448 different locomotive types in all.

A major priority was to recover from the years of wartime cutbacks, when the network had suffered from minimal investment.

Cometh the hour, cometh the man… Robert Arthur Riddles, who was appointed chief mechanical engineer of the newly formed Railway Executive.

Born on 23 May 1892, Riddles became an apprentice with the London & North Western Railway in 1909. He served with the Royal Engineers during WWI.

In 1933, Riddles became locomotive assistant to the LMS railway's new chief mechanical engineer, William Stanier and, in 1935, graduated to becoming his principal assistant.

At the outbreak of WWII, Riddles moved to the Ministry of Supply, becoming its director of transportation equipment. He designed the War Department Austerity 2-8-0 tender engines, the WD Austerity 2-10-0s – the first locomotives of this wheel arrangement to run in Britain – and the Austerity 0-6-0 saddle tanks, which were predominantly built by Hunslet.

He moved to the post of chief stores superintendent at the LMS in 1943 and was promoted to the position of vice-chairman of the company the following year.

In the period following nationalisation, there was already much talk about modernising the system using diesel and electric traction, as had already happened to a large extent in the USA. Riddles was in no doubt that this would take place, just not overnight.

What was needed for British Railways was a new fleet of 'universal' steam locomotive types which, broadly speaking, could operate throughout the system in the short to medium term while plans and investment for their replacement by 'modern' traction were amassed.

Riddles began designing and building a set of 12 standard locomotive designs, referred to as the BR Standards.

The BR Standard class was held to incorporate the best practices of all of the 'Big Four' railway companies' locomotive designs, but observers have often commented on a marked bias towards LMS types.

The Standards were designed for simplicity, ease of maintenance, and the ability to burn poor-quality coal when necessary.

The first was outshopped in 1951, from Crewe Works, in the form of Britannia class Pacific No 70000 *Britannia*.

Swindon Works would also have its slice of the action, as another 998 Standard locomotives were to be built, while constructing of 'Big Four' types such as the Modified Halls and panniers would be phased out. As it happened, British Railways still built 1538 steam locomotives to pre-nationalisation designs.

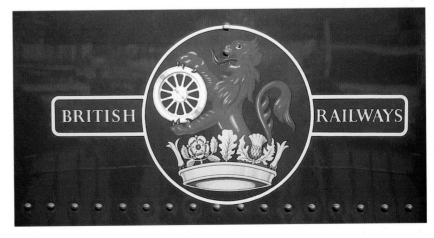

Also in 1951, British Railways introduced its Standard 4 4-6-0 tender locomotives.

They bore more than passing similarities to the Manors, although unlike them, they were built to a universal loading gauge.

Riddles undertook the design work at the Southern Region's Brighton Works, with assistance from works at Swindon, Derby, and Doncaster.

Swindon took responsibility for their construction, and 80 were built.

The class had two cylinders, 5ft 8in diameter driving wheels and was capable of a 25,500lb tractive effort, with a power classification of 4MT.

The class saw service on the London Midland, Southern as well as the Western Regions.

The first of the class, No 75000, had been painted in lined black mixed-traffic livery.

In 1957, after No 75029 was successfully modified with double blast pipes and a double chimney, it was repainted in the Swindon green livery, which had been introduced the year before. It was announced that all other members of the class would be similarly repainted, but this was never done.

Swindon had been yearning since 1948 to restore some semblance of GWR style.

After nationalisation, British Railways experimented with a variety of liveries for locomotives and stock.

Early in 1949 it was announced that the most powerful express passenger engines were to be painted in Caledonian Railway-style blue, with black and white lining. Several Kings were reliveried in this style – selected express passenger engines were to be dark GWR Brunswick green, with black and orange lining – while other passenger and mixed-traffic engines were to be

black, with red, cream and grey lining, and goods locomotives were to be plain black. The blue livery was soon abandoned. However, in the late 1950s, a new approach emerged, with a feeling that nationalised industries would perform well with more autonomy.

This U-turn delighted the Western Region, which accordingly applied the lined green livery to many of its classes that had not carried it before.

Six of the splendid Standard 4 4-6-0s are still with us today, in preservation: Nos 75014, 75027, 75029, 75069, 75078 and 75079.

Swindon designed the Standard Class 3 2-6-2 tank engine, although it was largely based on LMS practice with a boiler similar to a GWR No 2 type.

Most of the 45 members of the class worked on the Western Region, while some entered Southern Region service.

Many observers have commented that they were the ideal locomotive for economic operation of short- to medium-sized branch lines, and would be perfect for today's heritage and tourist railways.

Sadly, none survived into preservation, although a project to build what would have been the next off the production line, No 82045, is gathering pace at the Severn Valley Railway, with a set of frames delivered in spring 2007.

Another Riddles' design that was built at Swindon was the Standard Class 3 2-6-0, a tender engine version of the Standard 3 tank.

Just 20 of them were built, the boiler design being based on the Swindon No 2 type. Mainly running on the North Eastern and Scottish Regions, none have survived into preservation.

As well as the BR Standards, Swindon also built at least one other 'Big Four' company's design in the

post-war period, in the form of 25 examples of an LMS Class 2 2-6-0 tender engine.

George Ivatt, son of Great Northern Railway's locomotive engineer Henry Ivatt, became the post-war chief mechanical engineer of the LMS, and was called on to produce a new class of medium-powered locomotive.

As well as the 2-6-0, he came up with a tank engine version based on the GWR 4500 and 4575 classes.

Of the tender engines, 128 were built between 1946 and 1953, the majority at Crewe, others at Doncaster, and the first 20 by the LMS.

British Railways built the remaining engines using a slightly modified design with a slightly cut-down cab and BR Standard fittings.

The Swindon-built examples were first painted in lined black, but later received lined green livery as they passed through the works.

Out of seven of the tender engines, which survive in preservation, two were built in Swindon, No 46512 at the Strathspey Railway and No 46521 at the Great Central Railway. ∎

Introduced in 1964, the Standard 3MT 2-6-0 was a tender version of the Standard 3 tank engine also built at Swindon, of which only 20, including this example, No 77001, the second of the class were built. BRITISH RAIL

Opposite top: BR Standard 3MT 2-6-2 tank engine No 82024 engages in shunting duties while acting as Exeter Central station pilot on 11 May 1958. BRIAN MORRISON

Opposite middle: BR Standard 4MT No 75073 emerges from Swindon Works in mint condition following completion on 6 November 1955. BRIAN MORRISON

Opposite bottom: BR Standard 4MT 4-6-0 No 75029 passing Abbot House south of Goathland on the North Yorkshire Moors Railway, Britain's most popular heritage line carrying around 300,000 passengers a year, on 22 April 2006. The locomotive was named *The Green Knight* by international wildlife artist David Shepherd who bought the locomotive along with BR Standard 9F No 92203 from British Railways, and founded the East Somerset Railway so he had somewhere on which to run them. BRIAN SHARPE

Swindon-built Ivatt 2-6-0 No 46521 heading a Severn Valley Railway service train at Highley during the line's September 1980 gala. The locomotive is currently stored out of service on the Great Central Railway at Loughborough. In the background is Western diesel hydraulic D1062 *Western Courier*, built at Crewe to a Swindon design. BRIAN SHARPE

Painted by Terence Cuneo for the cover of the Unilever magazine 'Progress' Winter issue 1957-8

DIESELISATION

Going it alone again

While the GWR became respected internationally because of the widespread success of its Swindon-built locomotives, from early days it had been looking beyond steam. Brunel had infamously installed atmospheric traction on his South Devon Railway, running engineless trains between Exeter and Newton Abbot during 1847-48, before component failure led to the line's directors insisting the route be converted to steam haulage.

The atmospheric system involved trains being connected to a pipe, with steam-powered stationary engines installed in pumping houses at regular intervals along its length to draw the air out and thus create a vacuum. It was reported that speeds of up to 64mph were attained.

Brunel had, wrongly as it turned out, believed that the steep gradients of the route, the notorious South Devon banks such as Hemerdon and Rattery, would prove too great for steam, and as always, was predicting a future when it would be superseded.

It may well be that the atmospheric system was ahead of its time but was hindered by the contemporary materials available to create it. While sound in principle, the leather flap, which sealed the vacuum pipe perished in the salty coastal air, and was also said to have been gnawed by rats.

In 1934, the GWR pioneered the regular use of

railcars, built by London firm AEC, on cross-country services. These early railcars remained in service until the 1960s and pre-empted the widespread use of diesel and electric multiple units across the national network.

The USA had opted for dieselisation as early as the 1930s, and it was the rude interruption of WWII, which, logic dictates, held Britain back in this, and many other fields of modernisation. It is fascinating to conjecture what diesel locomotives would have been drawn up by the Swindon designers had nationalisation not taken place in 1948.

Following the development of its 350/400hp diesel shunters, the LMS was the first British railway company to introduce main line diesel-electric locomotives, in the form of Derby-built Nos 10000/10001, which were outshopped in December 1947.

The other major pioneer in the field of diesel-electric traction, the Southern Region, introduced the first of its prototypes, No 10201, in December 1950. The performance of these early machines was hampered by the conditions under which they were forced to operate; a rare diesel operating on a steam-

dominated network was a nuisance, and difficult to fix when failures occurred.

Following nationalisation, the BTC, which controlled the railways, wanted dieselisation, but met with resistance, and so British Railways built its 12 Standard classes. However, they would be little more than a stop-gap measure, for in 1955, British Railways announced its Modernisation Plan.

The newly nationalised railway network in 1948 had recorded a profit of £19-million, but by 1955 this had reversed to a deficit of £17-million. The car was well on its way to becoming king, bringing individual freedom of movement to the masses, while a crippling national rail strike drove many regular passengers from the railways that would never return. Something had to be done to make the railways attractive again.

The Modernisation Plan, which called for the eradication of steam and its replacement by diesel and electric traction may have been the right answer at the right time, but its implementation was little short of a disaster.

The report called for the introduction of 2500 locomotives with initial orders for 171 machines. The estimated cost of £1.24-billion was to be spread over

The first of the Kings, No 6000 *King George V*, meets with one of its 'replacements' Warship D821 *Onslaught*, at Swindon on 19 May 1979. BRIAN SHARPE

15 years, but this figure was greatly exceeded.

Instead of introducing proven standard designs of American construction, British Railways placed the orders for its diesel Pilot Scheme with home-based manufacturers.

Worse still, batches of 10 or 20 locomotives were ordered without a prototype locomotive being built first. Some of the early types were indeed successful, but others ended up being withdrawn before the last steam locomotives on the network.

Just as Brunel had doggedly forged ahead with his broad gauge in the face of national calls for 4ft 8½in to become the national standard, so the Western Region continued the GWR's fierce spirit of independence by going it alone a century on.

Instead of following the other regions in going down the line of diesel-electric traction, Western Region officials instead opted for diesel hydraulic.

In 1953-54, before the Modernisation Plan was published, several Western Region executives visited the continent to see the first of a new breed of high-powered main line diesel hydraulics, the V200 series, which entered service with the German Federal Railways in 1953.

At the same time, the North British Locomotive Company of Glasgow obtained licences to build German Voith hydraulic transmissions and MAN high-speed diesel engines.

After the Modernisation Plan had been published, Swindon representatives again went to Germany, and were impressed. It was calculated that the reduction in locomotive weight by using diesel-hydraulic rather

than diesel-electric traction meant an increase in haulage weights of an extra coach or two, and it was assumed that a lighter locomotive would also be cheaper to build.

It was agreed with British Railways that the Western Region could concentrate on diesel-hydraulic types, with design and building based at Swindon with some construction taking place at other establishments.

The BTC had already agreed to order two types of diesel-hydraulic locomotives from North British, a Type 4 A1A-A1A locomotive with two engines capable of producing 2000hp that became the D600 Warship series (six built) and a Type 2 Bo-Bo locomotive with a single engine producing 1000hp that became the D6300 'Baby Warships' (58 eventually built).

The advantage of lightweight construction was lost on these; however, as North British had no experience in stressed-skin body construction and changed the chassis design criteria.

The Western Region wanted neither of the North British types, but the BTC allocated them to it all the same.

The Western Region subsequently contacted the manufacturers of the V200, Krauss-Maffei, to begin designing a British version. The German V200 had to be scaled down to fit the British loading gauge, and Swindon designers eventually produced a Bo-Bo 2200hp design using two Maybach engines, Mekydro hydraulic transmission and a lightweight stressed-skin body enabling the desired high power-to-weight ratio to be achieved.

British Rail blue days: days Class 52 No 1010 *Western Campaigner* passes Iver on 13 April 1976. PAUL CHANCELLOR

In 1956, production of diesel locomotives in Britain exceeded that of steam for the first time.

D800 was the first main line diesel locomotive to be built by BR at Swindon and, constructed almost entirely by hand in the works, was completed in July 1958.

Entering traffic, it was named *Sir Brian Robertson* during a ceremony held at Paddington on 14 July.

The next day, D800 took the 'Cornish Riviera' from Paddington to Plymouth, returning with the 4.10pm from Plymouth.

A total of 38 examples of the class, which also came to be known as Warships – they were named after naval vessels – were built at Swindon. The BTC annoyed the Western Region somewhat by ordering another 33 from North British.

Seasoned steam drivers did not take too kindly to the Swindon Warships (later Class 42) at first, as the bogie design meant they experienced rough riding at speeds in excess of 75mph, but after tests were carried out in 1959-60 modifications were successfully introduced to overcome the problem.

On 27 July 1959, D807 *Caradoc* became the first diesel to haul the up 'Torbay Express'. Replacing steam on the service led to the down-working being cut by 10 mins to 165 mins between London and Exeter; the fastest time ever recorded between the cities.

The D800 class turned out to be a magnificent performer, capable of exceeding the authorised top speed of 90mph.

Sadly, while the D800s were being built – and production of steam locomotives continued alongside them at Swindon – the BTC was also ordering diesel-electric types from other manufacturers. As a result, British Railways ended up with an assortment of non-standard types that proved difficult to service if they strayed from their home region.

The immense wastage of taxpayers' money over the Pilot Schemes was finally realised when British Railways introduced a rationalisation policy.

In 1964 it was decreed that because of the relatively expensive costs of maintaining diesel hydraulics, diesel-electric traction was to be the norm.

A rationalisation policy, which appeared three years later in the form of the National Traction Plan, in 1967 called for all diesel hydraulics to be phased out. Of the 2976 main line diesels in service at that time, only 309 were diesel hydraulics.

So, 10 years after the D800s appeared, the first members of the class were withdrawn, and all had disappeared by 1972.

That is, save two, which were bought privately for preservation. D821 *Greyhound*, built at Swindon in 1960, is now based on the Severn Valley Railway, while 1961-built sister D832 *Onslaught*, outshopped from the works the following year, and the last of the class to be withdrawn by British Rail is on the East Lancashire Railway.

A third example survived into preservation. D818 *Glory* was displayed at Swindon as a static exhibit, but because its exterior condition had deteriorated, it was cut up in 1985. However, many of its parts were bought as spares for the other two survivors. ■

The Western diesel hydraulics

The Western Region's second Swindon-built diesel hydraulic type, the D1000 Western class, was much more of a home-grown affair than the D800 Warships. Swindon engineers looked at the design of Krauss-Maffei's experimental ML3000 3000bhp locomotive, which used the same Maybach MD650 engines and Mekydro K184 transmissions as the D800 class, but uprated to 1500hp.

However, this time round, the Western Region decided to design its own locomotive, utilising Maybach MD655 engines of 1380bhp and Voith L360rV transmissions, with the same stressed-skin method of body construction that had been used so successfully in the Swindon Warships.

A decision was also made to spread the workload among the various British Railways' suppliers. The engines were to be built by Bristol Siddeley Engines at Ansty, while 103 transmissions would be supplied by North British and Voith Engineering of Glasgow, with another 60 sets coming from Germany.

The BTC ordered 74 of what became known as the Westerns in 1959, splitting the order between Swindon and Crewe.

However, problems with the final design led to the first member of the class, D1000 *Western Enterprise*, not being delivered until December 1961, and to relieve pressure on Swindon, the final five earmarked for building at the works were instead built at Crewe. The Swindon-built Westerns – which later became Class 52 – were numbered D1000-29.

It was first intended to name the class after West Country beauty spots, with the first, D1000, becoming *Cheddar Gorge*, but this was quietly dropped in favour of *Western Enterprise*, and subsequent locomotives followed suit.

The class, one of the most stylish diesel locomotives to be built in Britain, became the subject of livery experiments. D1000 was outshopped in a unique desert sand livery with wheels, roof panels, bogies and window frames in black, and the buffer beams and front skirts in carmine red.

D1001 *Western Pathfinder*, was delivered in a maroon livery with white window frames and yellow buffer beams and front skirts. The next three, D1002-4, emerged in GWR Brunswick green but with small yellow panels applied around the headcodes.

D1001 *Western Pathfinder* outside its Swindon Works birthplace on 24 March 1963. GWR TRUST COLLECTION

D1015 *Western Champion* was outshopped in golden ochre with the buffer beams painted red. In preservation, it carried this livery when it returned to the main line in late 2001 following a major rebuild, being repainted maroon in 2006.

After D1000 entered traffic, it was sent to Plymouth Laira for trials, while in February 1962, D1001 was chosen to undertake trials in competition against the experimental locomotive D0280 *Falcon*, built by Brush Traction at Loughborough as the prototype of what would become the 512 Class 47s.

Unsatisfactory riding led to all but four of the Westerns being restricted to 80mph, but following a programme of bogie modifications, most of the type members were restored to working at 90mph by spring 1964.

With early problems ironed out, by the late 1960s, the Westerns were in top form, and although they were still despised by steam diehards, they had effectively replaced Collett's Kings on the Paddington system.

Their bogies were giving 150,000 miles between general repairs while the Voith transmission was shown to be a more reliable unit compared with the D800's Mekydro equivalent.

The rationalisation policy of 1967 earmarked this splendid class for withdrawal, but it managed to survive for another decade, at first owing to the unavailability of sufficient numbers of the West of England main line replacement, the English Electric Class 50 diesel electrics.

The Westerns were not fitted with electric train heating, and therefore could not power British Rail's new air-conditioned Mark IID coaches. That was a serious drawback at a time when, following the completion of the M4 between London and Bristol, British Rail was facing serious competition for its inter-city service from road traffic.

The Westerns, however, were excellent goods as well as passenger locomotives, working much heavy freight in South Wales, including the overnight Freightliner from Cardiff to London (Stratford), as well as overnight milk and cream workings from Devon and Cornwall.

In 1976, the survivors were officially relegated to freight duties, but became enormously popular with enthusiast specials to destinations across the country.

Only 10 remained at the start of 1977, and D1013 *Western Ranger* and D1023 *Western Fusilier* hauled the sell-out enthusiasts special the 'Western Tribute' on 26 February of that year. The last five Westerns were withdrawn two days later, and their passing marked the end not only of diesel hydraulics from the main line, but Swindon's spirit of independence. These five survived into preservation, along with another two, while most of the rest were cut up at Swindon.

Swindon-built examples still with us are D1010 *Western Campaigner* (West Somerset Railway, sometimes masquerades as D1035 *Western Yeoman*), D1013 *Western Ranger* (Severn Valley Railway), D1015 *Western Champion* (Old Oak Common, the only one certified for use on Network Rail) and D1023 *Western Fusilier* (National Railway Museum). The other survivors are D1041 *Western Prince* (East Lancashire Railway), D1048 *Western Lady* (Midland Railway Centre) and D1062 *Western Courier* (Severn Valley Railway). ■

Evening Star powers through Leamington with an enthusiast railtour on 13 September 1981. BRIAN SHARPE

Best saved for last

The 9F 2-10-0 has been widely praised as the most successful of all the 12 British Railways' Standard types – yet whether this class should have been built at all in the face of impending dieselisation remains debatable.

Designed by Robert Riddles, the first 9F was outshopped in 1954. The following year, the British Railways' Modernisation Plan was published, sounding the death knell for steam. In that case, why were 251 9Fs built, at a time when diesel and electric traction had been publicly confirmed as the sole way forward?

The 9Fs were built with a life expectancy of up to 40 years, yet British Railways was to decree that steam haulage on the national network would cease in 1968.

No 92210, for example, was therefore in service for just five years before withdrawal and scrapping, while No 92004, which enjoyed the longest run, lasted 14 years. It is often claimed that the class was never given a real chance to show its true potential.

Compare and contrast the British policy of dieselisation with that of West Germany, where Pacifics ran alongside state-of-the-art diesels until the mid-1980s.

Just as British Railways rushed into the diesel Pilot Schemes with mixed results, producing many unwanted types and wasting colossal amounts of public money, was the ending of steam as early as 1968 simply a point-of-principle move which saw perfectly serviceable locomotives scrapped with just a few miles on the clock?

The cost of building a class 9F rose by nearly 50 per cent during the six years it was in production, from around £24,000 in 1954 to nearly £34,000.

Hauling a rake of GWR liveried chocolate-and-cream coaches, *Evening Star* heads towards Williton on the West Somerset Railway on 7 September 1987. BRIAN SHARPE

While most of the 9Fs were built at Crewe, 43 of them were constructed at Swindon.

The first, No 92000, emerged from Crewe in January 1954 and the initial eight were allocated to the Western Region for use on South Wales' coal traffic.

The old Western hands did not like them at first, and experienced problems with the steam brake after standing, and a regulator that stuck open. Complaints were such that the region was not allocated any more until 1958, but nonetheless, the 9Fs proved very popular and successful elsewhere, especially on the Tyne Dock-Consett ore trains in the north-east, as well as the Shotton steel trains in North Wales.

Apart from the War Department Austerity 2-10-0s built during WWII, the 9F was the only locomotive type with this wheel arrangement built for service in Britain.

Designed as a no-nonsense heavy freight locomotive, class members also saw occasional passenger service, including summer Saturday duties. A Swindon-built example, No 92184 reached 90mph

on Stoke Bank in Lincolnshire during one such turn on 16 August 1958 with the 'Heart of Midlothian'.

The legendary Somerset & Dorset Joint Railway main line between Bath Green Park and Bournemouth West famously saw 9Fs in service on passenger trains in its latter days.

The route over the Mendip Hills was notorious for its 1-in-50 gradients, which required double heading, but a 9F could tackle them with ease – a huge bonus in the peak holiday season when crew numbers were low. Accordingly, four 9Fs were allocated to the route for several years.

Swindon Works had the honour of building the last steam locomotive for use on the British main line, No 92220 *Evening Star*, unveiled on 18 March 1960.

When *Evening Star* rolled off the production line, it brought to an end a proud tradition of steam building at Swindon that had begun with the construction of Daniel Gooch's *Great Western* 114 years earlier.

The works made sure that the occasion would never be forgotten.

The last steam locomotive to be built for British Railways, Standard 9F 2-10-0 No 92220 *Evening Star* is officially named at Swindon Works on 18 March 1960. PAUL CHANCELLOR

No 92220, which cost £33,500 to build, was painted in passenger green livery (all other 9Fs were painted unlined black), its external pipe work made in copper and brass and its double chimney given a copper cap.

The name *Evening Star* was decided through a competition and was the choice of three Western Region workers: Mr Phillips, a driver based at Aberystwyth, Mr Pugh, a clerk in the general manager's office at Paddington; and Mr Sathi, a boiler washer at Old Oak Common. They realised that *Morning Star* was one of the first locomotives to run on the Great Western Railway, being supplied by Robert Stephenson before Daniel Gooch built his own, and so *Evening Star* would be a fitting finale to the steam age.

In a moving speech at the naming ceremony, Western Region chairman Reggie Hanks, a former Swindon Works' apprentice said: "There had to be a last steam locomotive, and it is a tremendous thing that that last steam locomotive should be built here in these great works at Swindon.

"I am sure it has been truly said that no other product of man's mind has ever exercised such a compelling hold upon the public's imagination as the steam locomotive.

"No other machine in its day has been a more faithful friend to mankind nor has contributed more to the growth of industry in this the land of its birth and indeed throughout the whole world."

Allocated to the Western Region, Cardiff Canton depot regularly used No 92220 on the 'Red Dragon' express to Paddington. When the engine operated the

'Capitals United' express between Cardiff and London in July 1960, it also reached 90mph.

Evening Star too worked over the Somerset & Dorset line: it was chosen to haul the last of the route's most famous named train, the 'Pines Express' from Manchester to Bournemouth on 8 September 1962.

Evening Star was withdrawn from service in March 1965, but because of its historical importance, became part of the National Collection.

It was externally restored at Crewe Works in 1966-67 and placed in store at Preston Park in January 1968.

In June 1973, it was loaned to Yorkshire's Keighley & Worth Valley Railway, one of the earliest steam heritage lines which had shot to international stardom three years earlier when it was used for the location filming of the EMI big-screen production of E Nesbit's classic *The Railway Children* starring Jenny Agutter.

Evening Star was steamed on arrival at the line and worked there during 1974-75 before making a triumphant comeback to the main line.

Its first heritage-era railtour saw it run from Leeds to Grange-over-Sands and return on 31 May 1975. The locomotive was transferred to the custody of the NRM at York on 31 August that year.

It went on to operate railtours out of York, to Scarborough and over scenic upland route, the Settle & Carlisle line.

Evening Star was loaned to the Great Western Society at Didcot on 11 July 1980 and overhauled, resteaming in September the following year and returning to York in May 1983.

No 92220 worked railtours until September 1988, and then briefly worked on the West Somerset Railway – now at 24 miles Britain's longest independent steam line – from March 1989 until April 1990.

The locomotive returned to its Swindon birthplace in 1990, for static display, as part of the NRM on tour exhibition. While the York museum was being refurbished, many items from the National Collection were displayed at Swindon Works.

Evening Star is now on static display at the NRM, with no plans afoot to return it to steam.

Other Swindon-built 9Fs can, however, be seen in action today. No 92203 *Black Prince*, bought in the 1960s by international wildlife artist David Shepherd, is now a regular performer on the Gloucestershire Warwickshire Railway. There are also plans to return No 92212, now owned by city businessman Jeremy Hosking and based at the Mid-Hants Railway, to the main line.

Sadly the penultimate member of the class, No 92219, is a rusting heap of metal at the Midland Railway, Butterley, where the owning group has restored No 92214 to running order. There are no plans to restore it, despite is historical significance: it may end up as a source of spare parts to keep its sister running.

Another Swindon 9F, No 92207, named *Morning Star* in preservation, is being slowly restored from a rusting hulk at Shillingstone station on the former Somerset & Dorset line, maintaining a presence of the class on the route.

One of the Crewe-built examples, No 92240, is based on the Bluebell Railway, while No 92134 is being restored for use on the Churnet Valley Railway, Staffs, and unrestored No 92245 is in the custody of the Barry Island Railway.

The last steam locomotive built in India, at Chittaranjan Locomotive Works in 1972, was named *Antim Sitara*, which means 'the last star'.

It is a common misconception that *Evening Star* was the last steam locomotive built in Britain. Not so: industrial types continued to be turned out by Hunslet of Leeds in the early 1960s, along with narrow gauge locomotives for export.

In 1964, Hunslet supplied two new Austerity 0-6-0 saddle tanks for colliery use: they were the last steam engines built for British use by a British manufacturer on traditional commercial terms.

In 1971, Hunslet supplied an 0-4-2 saddle tank, works' number 3902, from its Leeds' factory to a sugar mill in Indonesia. It is held to be the last 'steam age' locomotive built in Britain. This 2ft gauge locomotive, *Trangkil No 4*, has since been reimported to Britain and restored to running order by Graham Lee, current owner of the modern-day Hunslet Engine Company, which is now building steam locomotives to historic designs at his private Statfold Barn Railway near Tamworth in Staffordshire, but for heritage rather than industrial use.

Riddles retired as mechanical engineer with the Railway Executive the year it was abolished in 1953. He became a director of cranemaker Stothert & Pitt of Bath, and died on 18 June 1983. ■

Evening Star was immortalised by the late Terence Cuneo, who many still regard as the greatest of all railway painters.

Class 14 D9555, the last locomotive of the class was also the last locomotive built by Swindon Works for use in Britain and was an obvious preservation candidate when it became available in 1987. It is currently based on the Dean Forest Railway where it was seen on December 3 2005 when it took part in the celebratory reopening of Parkend station as the line was extended from Norchard to give a through Lydney to Parkend run. FRED KERR

DIESEL HYDRAULICS

'Teddy Bears' *without a picnic*

One final type of diesel hydraulic was built at Swindon – the Class 14 0-6-0 centre-cab 650hp shunters, affectionately referred to by enthusiasts as 'Teddy Bears'. Basically designed for shunting operations, the 56-member class could also undertake short main line duties or trip workings with a speed of up to 40mph.

However, built between 1964 and 1965, they were born too late.

In between the time British Rail had ordered them and when they rolled off the Swindon production line, most of the work for which they had been designed had been lost in the post-Beeching era.

Class members were painted in two-tone green, the cab being a light green and the nose sections a darker shade.

Several were deployed on pick-up freights in the Gloucester and South Wales areas.

In late 1967, only two years after the last examples had been delivered, withdrawals began, and by 1969, all had disappeared off BR's books.

They were sold into industry, where many of them gave sterling service, at diverse locations ranging from National Coal Board colliery lines to a steel works in Brescia in Italy. A total of 23 have survived into the preservation era.

The other major Western Region diesel-hydraulic type, the Class 35 Bo-Bo Hymek, was built by Beyer Peacock in Manchester. Out of 101 built, four have survived into preservation. ■

This Swindon-built Class 03, D2192, which dates from 1962, has recently been reliveried into black by its owner the Paington & Dartmouth Steam Railway, where it has been named *Arden*.
DART VALLEY RAILWAY PLC

Swindon's *smallest diesels*

One of the largest classes of locomotive type built by Swindon in post-war years was also the smallest type – the British Railways' Class 03 shunter.

A 'small' standard shunting locomotive was needed for the post-steam network, British Railways having either inherited or ordered a motley assortment of different types from different manufacturers.

It was decided to go for a small-to-medium wheelbase 0-6-0 design, fitted with a diesel-mechanical transmission, and in 1955 the British Railways Workshops Division contracted the mechanical assembly to both Swindon and Doncaster Works.

A total of 230 of the type were built, 146 of them at Swindon, between December 1957 and June 1962.

Herein lies an amusing tale. Drawing on the century-old Swindon spirit of independence, the works' manager decided that the shunters would not only carry steam locomotive-style chimneys, but also have a GWR-style copper cap!

He was overruled by British Railways, which instead ordered the exhaust 'chimney' or stack to be of a conical design. In practice, this proved inadequate, as the light weight at the nose end caused adhesion problems.

The solution was to fit a heavy metal surround to the exhaust stack, based on a steam locomotive design!

The entire fleet was outshopped in British Railways' green, with British Rail corporate blue applied from 1967 onwards.

With the end of the pick-up goods, which had typified country branch lines, and the closure of freight yards across the country, the 230-strong fleet was found to be too big for the needs of the national network.

The 03s were withdrawn from the middle of the 1960s onwards, many being eagerly snapped up by industrial concerns, and later, dozens found new homes on preserved railways.

The last 03 in network service was in operation at the Hornsey depot in north London, No 03179, still at work in the 21st century. ∎

The age of the *diesel railcar*

At what may have been considered the height of the steam age, in 1933 the GWR introduced diesel railcars on parts of its network.

The idea of a self-contained self-propelled passenger-carrying vehicle was, of course, not new: the GWR was one of several pre-Grouping companies which had used steam railmotors, with a steam locomotive 'built into' one end of the carriage, the pair being either combined on a single underframe or articulated together.

Alongside the steam railmotor concept was the auto-train, immortalised by Collett's 14XX 0-4-2 tank engines and their auto-trailers. Their 'push-pull' working saw special carriages fitted with a driver's compartment at one end, so it was possible to control the steam locomotive pushing it from the other, with just the fireman remaining on the engine footplate, eradicating the need for run-round operations and

thereby speeding up times on branch line journeys. In some instances the engine was placed in the centre of the train, with the train being able to be driven from the cabs at both ends of the stock.

The idea of powering railmotors with an internal combustion rather than steam engine led to several trials in the pre-Grouping era.

One classic example that, hopefully, we might enjoy again is the North Eastern railway petrol-electric railcar built in York in 1902 and introduced the following year by the Northern Eastern Railway. One of a pair, No 3170 was withdrawn from service in 1931, sold off for use as a shed, and is now the subject of a rebuilding scheme by acclaimed Yorkshire carriage restorer Stephen Middleton.

The diesel railcar concept took the idea one step further, and sowed the seeds for a multitude of different types, both of single units and diesel-multiple units, which dominate today's network at a

Preserved Swindon-built GWR railcar W22W on the running line at its Didcot Railway Centre home.
PAUL CHANCELLOR

time when locomotive-hauled passenger trains are a rarity.

The GWR railcar was invented by CF Cleaver of Hardy Railmotors Ltd, a subsidiary of the Associated Equipment Co Ltd (AEC).

Cleaver realised that the 130bhp six-cylinder AEC diesel engine, which had proved so successful in London buses and other commercial vehicles, was capable of powering a lightweight self-contained railcar, especially if it utilised aerodynamic streamlining.

The body of the first prototype was based on the Deutsche Reichsbahn 'Flying Hamburger' diesel unit. However, after undergoing wind tunnel tests at the Chiswick laboratory of the London Passenger Transport Board, it underwent a transformation into an 'art deco' streamlined design.

Park Royal Coachworks of Willesden, another AEC subsidiary, built the 69-seater body and the finished vehicle had a maximum speed of 63mph with control shared between the ends of the railcar.

The GWR bought the railcar before it was completed, and displayed it at the International Commercial Motor Transport Exhibition at Olympia in November 1933, generating immense public interest. Its rounded lines led to its 'Flying Banana' nickname, but later examples had a more angular shape.

The first official journey of Railcar No 1, from Paddington to Reading, took place on 1 December 1933, entering public service three days later, working from Slough shed to Windsor and Didcot. It completed 60,000 miles and carried 136,000 passengers in its first year.

The GWR was so delighted that it ordered six of the railcars from AEC. A number of improvements were made to the design, including the instalment of two AEC 8.85ltr diesel engines, thus raising the maximum speed to 80mph.

The three units were to be fitted with a buffet bar for use as an express businessmen's service between Birmingham and Cardiff.

These three entered regular service on 16 July 1934. They formed the first regular diesel working to be run to a fast schedule in Britain with the 117½ miles between Birmingham and Cardiff being covered in two hours and 20 mins.

A total of 38 of these railcars eventually appeared,

with several variations including parcel cars and examples fitted with drawgear for hauling vans.

Nos 2-4 were built by Park Royal, with Nos 5-18 constructed by the Gloucester Carriage & Wagon Co Ltd, and Nos 19-38 at Swindon.

At first used on cross-country routes, they soldiered on into the 1960s on branch line duties. Three have survived into preservation, including Swindon, 1940-built W20W at the Kent & East Sussex Railway and W22W at Didcot Railway Centre, with Park Royal, 1934-built W4W at the STEAM Museum of the Great Western Railway.

The success of the GWR railcars, especially in the difficult conditions of post-war Britain, did not go unnoticed. A committee established after nationalisation in 1948 to examine future motive power requirements recommended in 1952 that the diesel railcar should be developed for local and branch line services, as it had the potential to help keep many loss-making routes open.

Above: A Class 124 DMU built at Swindon Works passed Chaloner's Whin on 30 April 1977.

Top: A Class 120 diesel multiple unit in service at Shrewsbury on 13 June 1982. FRED KERR

Below: An example of the now-extinct Class 123 DMU at Reading on 13 September 1975. FRED KERR

The only surviving Swindon-built DMU set, a Class 126 unit, is under restoration by the Scottish Railway Preservation Society. SRPS

The Government then endorsed the spending of £1.5-million on two-car diesel-multiple units, which emerged as the first eight Derby-built 'lightweight' sets in 1954.

Next year came the Modernisation Plan, which gave the BTC the means to invest in 4600 diesel railcars and multiple units.

In order to rush the new units into service, they were commissioned from both the existing British Railways' workshops – including Swindon – as well as private companies, with the result that there was a marked variation in types from the standard stipulated.

The Swindon 'cross-country' two-car Class 120 diesel-multiple units, which were mainly used as three-car sets, were introduced in October 1957, and totalled 194 cars comprising 58 sets for the Western Region and seven for the Scottish Region, working mainly on the Aberdeen to Inverness line.

The class lasted in service until 1982, after which withdrawals followed, with the last in 1989. Just one vehicle survives; trailer No 59276, at the Great Central Railway in Loughborough, where it operates with two Class 127 power cars.

Swindon went on to design and build the 10 Class 123 three- or four-car diesel-multiple unit sets in 1963, totalling 40 vehicles. The design harked back to the British Railways' Mark I coaching stock, and had gangway connectors in front of the driving cabs.

At first based in Cardiff to operate Swansea-Birmingham-Derby services, after two years they were switched to the Cardiff-Bristol-Portsmouth route. Later they were used on Paddington-Oxford and Cardiff-Crewe services, and after another round of stock rationalisation in 1977, were transferred to Hull Botanic Gardens' depot to operate in conjunction with Class 124s on trans-Pennine services.

The Class 124s, introduced in 1960, were built by Swindon as six-car sets especially for the aforementioned trans-Pennine route from Neville Hill depot in Leeds, but ended their days as three-car sets. Fifty-one vehicles, including 17 of each driving motor composites and motor brake seconds, were built.

A unique class, its distinctive feature was the 'modern' wrap-round cab front windows, which proved expensive to build and replace.

Neither the Class 123s or 124s were selected by British Rail for 1980s refurbishment, mainly because of their non-standard design, and the last were withdrawn in 1984. Sadly, no vehicle from either set survived into preservation.

The Class 126 Swindon inter-city three- and six-car diesel-multiple units were designed for use on the Edinburgh Waverley to Glasgow Queen Street route at speeds of 70mph and built in 1956. However, the first six three-car sets worked their first three years on the Western Region on Birmingham-South Wales' services.

The works built a second batch in 1959-60 for use on services from Glasgow to Ayrshire, which is where the last two sets in operation on the network were withdrawn from service in January 1983.

In all, 45 power cars and 23 trailer vehicles were built.

Following withdrawal, five leading power cars were exported to Liberia for use by the LAMCO mining company for staff trains, and happily, four vehicles, Nos 51017, 51043, 59404 and 79443 survive in preservation.

They are owned by the Scottish Railway Preservation Society, based at the Bo'ness & Kinneil Railway, which has obtained £309,000 in grant aid from the Heritage Lottery Fund to rebuild a complete set. Thanks to these bodies, an important slice of both Scottish railway heritage and Swindon manufacturing history will survive for future generations. ∎

Swindon Class 126 Inter-City DMU No Sc51015 on the 12.35pm Glasgow Central to Aye service on 2 June 1977. BRIAN MORRISON

The Vale of Rheidol 2-6-2Ts

While Western Region steam – on 4ft 8½in gauge – ended in December, that was not the end of the story. Three Swindon-built steam engines remained in service, and apart from repairs or overhauling, have never been withdrawn for scrapping, nor are ever likely to be.

The trio run on the 1ft 11½in gauge Vale of Rheidol Railway, which runs for 11¾ miles, from Aberystwyth to the beauty spot of Devil's Bridge.

The line opened for mineral traffic in August 1902 and for passengers on 22 December of that same year.

In July 1913 the line was absorbed by the Cambrian Railways, which became part of the GWR at the Grouping of 1923. In turn, the Vale of Rheidol Railway became part of British Railways.

While steam on the main line ended in August 1968, British Rail decided to keep the little Welsh line open as a tourist attraction, painting its three engines in corporate blue livery, with the post-1965 double-arrow logo on each side.

These three locomotives, Nos 7 *Owain Glyndwr*, 8 *Llywelyn* and 9 *Prince of Wales*, all 2-6-2 tank engines,

had been built at Swindon in 1923-24.

No 7 was described as a 'rebuild' of the line's earlier No 2 (GWR No 1213), one of a pair built by Davies & Metcalfe of Manchester for the opening.

It has been said that the 'deception' of Swindon Works in supplying a new locomotive in the guise of a scrapped one came about because the GWR board had sanctioned only two new engines for the line.

At the same time, a Swindon design was used to build these two, which became Nos 8 and 9.

Under British Rail, the trio were even given a Total Operations Processing System (TOPS) class number, 98, just like standard gauge diesels.

Incidentally, TOPS, which has been employed on Britain's national network since 1972, is similar to the system of locomotive numbering used by the GWR, in which the class type, for example 28XX, is followed by the individual number.

The Vale of Rheidol Railway was sold privately in 1989, and now runs as a heritage line, the British Rail blue livery having long since gone, and GWR green reintroduced. ■

Wearing Great Western livery, Swindon-built Vale of Rheidol Railway 2-6-2T No 8 *Llewelyn* approaches Devil's Bridge with a train from Aberystwyth in August 2006. This classic narrow gauge railway was once part of the GWR empire. BRIAN SHARPE

Afterlife for steam

When 1929-built Great Western pannier tank No 5775 was bought for the Keighley & Worth Valley Railway from London Transport, where it had seen service on Underground works trains, it was repainted in a variery of 'freelance' liveries. One of the stars of the EMI big screen versiuon of Edith A Nesbit's classic *The Railway Children* which was filmed on the line and released in 1970, it was painted in an orange livery carrying the lettering of the fictitious Great Northern and Southern Railway. It is seen in 1990 leaving Ingrow heading a 20th anniversary special commemmorating the release of the film. BRIAN SHARPE

Until the middle of the 20th century, railway preservation had entailed the saving of a few select historical locomotives for static display in museums. Indeed, the first British engine to be saved for posterity was *Invicta*, the 1830-built pioneer locomotive, which ran on the Canterbury & Whitstable Railway, and was withdrawn in 1839. It is now on static display in Canterbury Heritage Museum.

As we have seen, 4-4-0 No 3440 *City of Truro* was preserved as a museum exhibit after withdrawal in 1931, only to later make a main line comeback in British Railways' service.

Sadly, the saving of classic obsolete locomotives for future generations was a rarity throughout the steam age.

When almost every other Brunel broad gauge locomotive was cut up after the final demise of the 7ft 0¼in system in 1892, two were set aside – *North Star*, the company's first locomotive, and the 4-4-2 *Lord of the Isles*. Disgracefully, in 1906, both were cup up at Swindon – on the orders of the works' manager – none other than locomotive designer extraordinaire-to-be William Stanier, who clearly didn't have the time or space for heritage locomotives.

Churchward, who was on holiday when this act of vandalism was committed, rescued parts from North Star, which were reassembled to create a static exhibit in 1925, and is now at the STEAM –

Museum of the Great Western Railway.

Lessons were not learned: in 1935, when the GWR marked its centenary, the South Devon Railway 2-4-0 broad gauge saddle tank *Prince*, converted to standard gauge in 1893, and used as a stationary heating boiler at Swindon Works after withdrawal in 1899, was cut up. Accordingly, all that was left of the once-world beating broad gauge fleet was a miniscule 0-4-0 vertical-boilered locomotive, *Tiny*, which had been built for the South Devon Railway, and is now on display inside the Buckfastleigh museum. This was tantamount to a civilisation in our distant future inheriting a 1960s bubble car as the sole-surviving example of 20th-century road transport!

While, however, the principle of saving locomotives for historical interest had been established, the concept of taking over a redundant railway and running it by volunteers had not become reality, at least not until the formation of the Talyllyn Railway Preservation Society. This society was set up following an exchange of correspondence in *The Birmingham Post* newspaper in September 1949 regarding the independent 2ft 3in gauge central Wales' line's impending demise.

The idea of private individuals taking over a railway was not new: it had been discussed when the 3ft gauge Southwold Railway in Suffolk closed in 1929, and again in 1941 just before the original Welsh

Highland Railway, following closure, had its track lifted for the war effort.

Under the leadership of transport author Tom Rolt, the volunteer-run Talyllyn Railway began operations in 1951, using two engines bought from its sister line, the closed Corris Railway, which, incidentally, had in 1930 become the last railway company to be absorbed by the GWR.

There were many who scoffed at the time: why save a steam railway for posterity, when the whole of Britain's railways was run by steam traction, barring all but a handful of experimental diesels?

The same year, a meeting was held in Bristol to form a society to reopen the closed 1ft 11½in gauge Ffestiniog Railway, which began its heritage-era services under volunteers three years later, headed by Alan Pegler, later to become famous as the man who bought *Flying Scotsman* from British Railways in 1963, saving it from the scrapyard.

During the 1950s, when it became obvious that the days of steam were numbered, interest in preserving locomotives and finding lines on which to run them grew.

Ironically, when the first standard, as opposed to narrow, gauge preserved or heritage railway was taken over by volunteers, its first services were hauled by a diesel locomotive. On 20-24 June, the freight-only Middleton Railway in Leeds, run by Leeds University

students under the leadership of lecturer the late Dr Fred Youell, operated its first passenger services, using a six-wheeled Hunslet diesel shunter pulling a Swansea and Mumbles Railway double-deck tramcar.

Shortly afterwards, the Bluebell Railway in Sussex ran its first trains. This was a real landmark in preservation, marking the first takeover of a section of closed British Railways' line by a volunteer group. Formed mainly by students under the chairmanship of Bernard Holden, a signalling assistant in the general manager's office at Liverpool Street station, its preservation society held its inaugural meeting at Haywards Heath in March 1959. Its first heritage-era train passenger traffic ran over the leased four-mile section of the East Grinstead to Lewes cross-country route between Sheffield Park and a point south of Horsted Keynes on 7 August 1960.

None of these schemes, however, had so far involved Swindon products.

However, with country branch lines facing the axe in the West Country, efforts were made to save the Moretonhampstead and then the Kingsbridge lines in vain.

Eventually, a group of businessmen who had the vision to realise that when the day came that steam trains would no longer run, the public would become nostalgic, and would be prepared to pay to ride on a line reopened as a tourist attraction.

Swindon steam still reigns supreme in torbay. A 10 May 2007 scene at Churston on Paignton & Dartmouth Steam Railway sees GWR prairie No 4555 passing between Western Region 4-6-0 No 7827 *Lydham Manor* and GWR 2-8-0 tank No 5239 *Goliath*, while working the 11.15am service from Kingswear. The boiler certificate of No 4555 expired a few days later, while No 5239 has emerged from the line's paint shop fully repainted, lined and lettered, ready for test steaming and running in following its ten-year overhaul. No 5239 and No 7827 will be the mainstays for service trains on this hugely-successful seaside heritage line for the next few years, assisted by pannier Paignton & Dartmouth Railway for the next few years, assisted by pannier tank No 6435 in the low season and during the peak summer service.
DVR

Castle class 4-6-0 No 5051 *Earl Bathurst* masquerades as scrapped sister No 5054 *Earl of Ducie* on 18 March 2007, during the west Somerset Railway's spring steam gala, during which a total of 10,375 passenger were carried over a six-day period. The event, which had a Summer Saturdfay in the West theme, was hailed as the most successful of its kind in the history of the British preservation movement. The revived 24-mile former Great Western Railway Minehead branch, once again a bastion of Swindon steam, is Britain's longest heritage railway. DON BISHOP

Forming Dart Valley Railway Ltd, the group took over the GWR Ashburton branch, which had closed to passengers in 1958, and to goods in 1962.

Sadly, the company had to give up the northern-most two miles between Buckfastleigh and Ashburton when the trackbed was needed for the conversion of the A38 into a dual carriageway. After difficulties in obtaining a Light Railway Order from the then Ministry of Transport, the first heritage-era trains ran over the line on 5 April 1969.

But a far more lucrative venture was to appear on the horizon. Western Region had decided to close the Paignton to Kingswear branch line, which, in effect,

was a single-track extension of the main line, and with its sweeping panoramic views of Torbay, it quickly found a ready buyer in the Dart Valley. The company took over the Kingswear line from 1 January 1972 without a break in service.

Serving the English Riviera of Torbay, the former GWR line has proved a huge success. However, in 1989 falling revenue led to the company announcing plans to close or sell off the original Buckfastleigh operation.

This stretch of line, an epitome of the classic West Country GWR branches, was taken over by the company's volunteer supporting association, and

Following a 77-day journey across the globe by sea, GWR 4-6-0 No 4079 *Pendennis Castle* is offloaded from cargo ship Toba at Portbury Docks near Bristol on 8 July 2000 after being repatriated from Australia. In 2007 it was being restored to main line running order at Didcot Railway Centre, for a second career in British preservation. ADRIAN KNOWLES

A wintry scene on the Severn Valley Railway painted by local multiple awardwinning railway artist John Austin. Great Western prairie No 5164 heads a passenger train into Bewdley, with pannier No 5764 waiting to the left and $-6-0 No 7802 *Bradley Manor* in the background.

became the South Devon Railway. In recent years, it has followed a policy of phasing out British Railways' stock to specialise in GWR locomotives and carriages.

Buckfastleigh is today home to eight GWR locomotives in Collett auto tank No 1420, 1366 class 0-6-0 pannier tank No 1369, Collett 2251 0-6-0 No 3205, 2884 2-8-0 No 3803, Hall 4-6-0 No 4920 *Dumbleton Hall*, 4500 prairie No 5526 and 5700 pannier No 5786.

The Kingswear line, now marketed as the Paignton & Dartmouth Steam Railway, and the only heritage line to pay a dividend to its shareholders, has five GWR-designed engines, in prairies Nos 4555 and 4588, 5205 class 2-8-0 tank No 5239, 6400 series pannier tank No 6435 and Manor 4-6-0 No 7827 *Lydham Manor*, which was built in Western Region days. Also on its stock list is Swindon-built British Railways' Standard 4MT 4-6-0 No 75014, which in preservation has been named *Braveheart*.

The success of the Bluebell Railway inspired West Midlands-based enthusiasts to look at the possibility of setting up a preserved line in their area, and on 6 July 1965, a meeting in the Cooper's Arms in Habberley, near Kidderminster, led to the formation of the Severn Valley Railway on part of the former GWR cross-country route that ran from Shrewsbury to Hartlebury Junction and Kidderminster.

The section from Bridgnorth to Hampton Loade was opened for public passenger services on 23 May 1970, with Collett's No 3205, then based on the line, hauling the first train. It was subsequently extended southwards in stages to Kidderminster, 16 miles away, where a new station, Kidderminster Town opened to passenger services on 30 July 1984. It is now, in terms

of passenger numbers, Britain's second-most popular heritage railway.

Its extensive GWR fleet comprises 2800 class 2-8-0 No 2857, prairies Nos 4150, 4566 and 5164, 5700 panniers Nos 5764 and 7714, 1500 class pannier No 1501, 4300 class mogul No 7325, Manors No 7802 *Bradley Manor*, No 7812 *Erlestoke Manor* and No 7819 *Hinton Manor* and Hall No 4930 *Hagley Hall*, pulls the sole-surviving Port Talbot Railway locomotive, an 0-6-0 saddle tank, which was not built at Swindon, but was taken into the GWR fleet at the Grouping and numbered 813.

Swindon-built designs for British Railways are represented by Standard 4MT 4-6-0 No 75069, Warship diesel hydraulic D821 *Greyhound* and

HRH The Princess Royal performed the official opening of the Gloucestershire Warwickshire Railway's extension to Cheltenham (Racecourse) on 7 April 2003. She is seen alongside Swindon, 1944-built Modifield Hall 4-6-0 No 6960 *Raveningham Hall* after chatting to the footplate crew. This heritage line has the ultimate ambition of rebuilding the 28-mile Great Western Railway route between Stratford-upon-Avon and Cheltenham which was closed by British Rail in 1976. ROBIN JONES

Didcot Railway Centre had humble beginnings, but now boasts the largest concentration of Brunswick green locomotives. Pictured left to right on 2 June 1985, during the Great Western 150 celebrations, are auto tank No 1466, heavy freight 2-8-0T No 5224 and 0-6-0ST No 1363.
BRIAN SHARPE

The Steel, Steam and Stars gala at the Llangollen Railway on 20-22 April 2007, sponsored by *Heritage Railway* magazine, brought together no less than nine nine Swindon designed or built locomotives for a landmark event to raise money to help build a new Grange 4-6-0. Led by Collett auto tank No 1450, a last evening cavalcade featured Hawksworth pannier No 9466, 2-8-0 tank No 5224, prairie No 4160, 0-6-2T No 5643, auto-fitted pannier No 6430, prairie No 5199, BR Standard 2MT 2-6-0 No 78019, No 7822 *Foxcote Manor*, heavy freight 2-8-0 No 3802 and Southern Railway Bulleid Pacific No 34081 *92 Squadron*.
CRAIG TILEY

Westerns Nos D1013 *Western Ranger* and D1062 *Western Courier*.

There are now more than 100 heritage railways in Britain, many of which came about largely through the success of these early pioneers. Swindon-built locomotives and stock can be seen on many of them, but space limitations here restrict us to the ones established in former GWR territory.

Britain's longest heritage line is the West Somerset Railway running over the 24-mile Minehead branch line, which was closed by British Rail in 1971, seven years after being used for the location for the Beatles' movie *A Hard Day's Night*.

It was reopened at Easter in 1976, initially running steam trains between Minehead and Blue Anchor, but regular passenger services were extended to Bishops Lydeard, the last station on the branch before the main line is reached, in 1979.

Upgrading of the main line connection at Norton Fitzwarren Junction in 2006 allowed regular running of through trains from the national network to the branch line for the first time since closure, although the line does not, at present, plan to operate its heritage services into Taunton.

The railway grows from strength to strength, in 2006 it won a third successive national award for being the best heritage railway in Britain. It now carries more than 200,000 passengers a year and has plans to build locomotive turning facilities at both ends, making it even more attractive for charter trips to come in from the main line.

Its GWR fleet comprises 2800 class 2-8-0 No 3850, prairies Nos 4160, 4561 and 5542, 6400 pannier No 6412, and three locomotives built at Swindon in British Railways days, Manor 4-6-0s Nos 7820 *Dinmore Manor* and 7828 *Odney Manor*, plus Western diesel hydraulic D1010 *Western Campaigner*.

The Dean Forest Railway Society was originally formed in 1970 to preserve the Lydney to Parkend branch of the Severn and Rye Railway, held its first steam open day the following year. Members developed a base at the former Norchard Colliery, and by 1978, a running line of 150 yards had been laid.

By 1995, services were running into the station at

Class 14 'Teddy Bears' D9516 and
D9523 take charge of a Nene Valley
Railway passenger train on 6
October 1990, when they are seen
passing Orton Mere.
BRIAN SHARPE

Lydney Junction, and in 2006, the present terminus of
Parkend was opened to passenger trains for the first
time since 1929. On 22 April 2007, the railway
accepted its first incoming steam charter from the
national network.

GWR-designed engines based on this 4½-mile line
comprise prairies Nos 5538 and 5541, and 5700
pannier No 9681. It was one of the routes over which
the short-lived Class 14s ran during their brief British
Railways' days in the 1960s, and one of them, D9555,
is based there today.

An operational GWR fleet is to be found at the
Bodmin & Wenford Railway, which runs two lines
between Bodmin General station and Boscarne and
Bodmin Parkway after being reopened in stages
between 1986 and 1996. Shedded there today are
5700 Class pannier No 4612, prairie No 5552 and 2-
8-0 tank No 4247.

While the above-mentioned preservation schemes
took place over railways that were intact, others have
had to lay track from new.

The Gloucestershire Warwickshire Railway runs
along a part of the GWR double-track main line
from Birmingham to Cheltenham via Stratford-
upon-Avon. Opened throughout in 1908, it was the
last of the company's major routes to be built.

'The Cornishman' express, complete with its
chocolate and cream coaches, ran over this railway
from 1952 until 1962 and formed the
Wolverhampton to Penzance service via Birmingham,
Stratford-upon-Avon, Cheltenham, Gloucester,
Bristol, Taunton, Exeter and Plymouth.

Stopping passenger services over the whole route
ceased in 1960, those from Stratford to Honeybourne
(and then on to Worcester) lingered on until 1969, and
the line remained open for freight until a derailment in
1976 caused track damage which British Rail did not
think was worth the expense in correcting.

On 22 April 1984 then transport secretary Nicholas
Ridley MP cut the ribbon to mark the official
reopening of the first quarter-mile of the line, which
ran from the revivalists' base at Toddington station,
and on 7 April 2003, the Princess Royal opened the
most recent extension, to Cheltenham Racecourse,
giving a total length of 10 miles.

GWR locomotives based on the line in 2007
included 2800 class 2-8-0 No 2807, 2-8-0 tank
engine No 4270, Halls Nos 6960 *Raveningham Hall*
and 6984 *Owsden Hall*, and Modified Hall No 7903
Foremarke Hall. The operational fleet included British
Railways' Standard 9F 2-10-0 No 92203, which was
also built at Swindon.

The Llangollen Railway Society was set up in 1977
by its predecessor, the Flint and Deeside Railway
Preservation Society, which had decided to restore
part of the GWR cross-country route between
Ruabon and Dolgellau, rebuilding westwards from
the tourist magnet of Llangollen.

The first heritage-era passengers were carried
between Llangollen and Fford Junction in 1981, and
by 1996, services had been extended in stages to
Carrog, a distance of 7½ miles, with a further
extension to Corwen being planned.

GWR-designed engines based or operating there
include 2800 class Nos 2859 and 3802, prairies
Nos 5199, 5532, 5538 and 5539, panniers Nos 6430
and 7754 and the line's flagship, No 7822 *Foxcote Manor*.

The East Somerset Railway, which runs over two
miles of the GWR Cheddar Valley line, is home to
GWR 0-6-2 tank No 5637, on loan from its owning
group, which is based at the Swindon & Cricklade
Railway, and is the preserved section of Swindon's
'other' railway, the Midland & South Western Junction
Railway that the GWR acquired at the Grouping.

Maintaining a Swindon presence at the 3½-mile
Chinnor & Princes Risborough Railway, Oxon, the
surviving part of the Watlington branch, is 1949-built
5700 pannier No 9682. It belongs to the GWR

Preservation Group, which in turn is trying to re-establish its museum at Southall.

Other heritage and tourist lines operating over GWR standard gauge trackbeds include the Cholsey & Wallingford Railway, Gwili Steam Railway, the Plym Valley Railway, the Telford Steam Railway (home of 1925-built 5600 class 0-6-2T No 5619), the Brecon Mountain Railway and the Lappa Valley Railway, the last two being narrow gauge.

However, the biggest single collection of GWR locomotives and rolling stock by far is to be found not on a 'typical' preserved railway, but at a museum with a series of demonstration running lines – Didcot Railway Centre. Herein lies one of the most remarkable stories of the preservation movement, one which began in 1961 when four schoolboys trainspotting at Southall decided to try to preserve a Collett 1400 tank, disappointed that one had been omitted from the BTC's list of engines to be saved for the proposed National Collection.

Their efforts led to the formation in 1964 of the Great Western Society, which not only succeeded in saving No 1466 but many others as well. At one stage

it had branch groups at places as diverse as Bodmin General and Totnes Quay, but after it was offered the use of the redundant steam shed at Didcot in 1967, all of the stock was collected under one roof.

Didcot had been briefly considered for the site of Brunel's great workshops before the final choice was made for Swindon. A glance in Didcot's sheds today will show that in terms of locomotive types, it is the richest example of 'Swindon in exile'.

Among the many other Swindon designs and builds there today are 1361 class saddle tank No 1363, 5700 panniers Nos 3650 and 3738, 2800 2-8-0 No 3822, Castles No 4079 *Pendennis Castle* and No 5051 *Earl Bathurst*, mogul No 5322, prairies Nos 5572 and 6106, Halls No 5900 *Hinderton Hall* and No 6998 *Burton Agnes Hall*, King No 6023 *King Edward II*, 7200 class 2-8-2T Manor No 7808 *Cookham Manor*, and GWR diesel railcar No 22.

More GWR engines were to survive into the heritage era than those turned out by any other 'Big Four' company, and it was all owing to a fateful decision made by one man, whose profession was the exact opposite of a preservationist. ∎

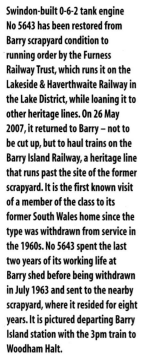

Swindon Works *after* 1986

The closure of Swindon Works by British Rail Engineering Ltd in 1986 left the great railway town devastated. However, the spirit of Brunel, Gooch, Churchward and Collett refused to die.

Chartered surveyor Bill Parker, an enthusiast since his boyhood days who had made his fortune in the USA, met up with old friend Ivor Huddy, a works' employee who had previously helped him to buy two steam locomotives.

The pair hatched a plan save at least part of the works so steam locomotives could continue to be maintained, and so they formed the Swindon Heritage Trust with other trustees including Bill Bradshaw, former Western Region general manager.

After British Rail sold the works' site to Tarmac Properties Bill agreed a deal with the company and the Swindon Railway Workshop was born, owned by Swindon Heritage Trust, which was allowed to occupy four acres of building space.

In 1989 it was becoming apparent that York's NRM would have to find a home for much of the National Collection while the roof of its main building was replaced. With some difficulty, Bill persuaded Tarmac Properties to allow the works to be used as its temporary home.

The 1990 'National Railway Museum on Tour' exhibition at Swindon saw masterpieces such as No 6000 *King George V* No 3440 *City of Truro* and No 92220 *Evening Star* displayed alongside Gresley's A4 Pacific No 4468 *Mallard*.

During that time Bill Parker had been introduced to the late Diana, Princess of Wales, who told him that her children William and Harry were "mad on trains", and inevitably an invitation to Swindon followed. The princes stayed for two hours: climbing up on the buffer beam of *King George V*, and riding precariously on the back of the works' traction engine up to *City of Truro*!

It had been hoped that the heritage version of Swindon Works would become permanent. However, when the 'Thatcher Boom' of the late 1980s burst and the value of commercial developments collapsed, Tarmac Properties gave Swindon Railway Workshop notice to quit.

Protests and bad publicity eventually forced a U-turn by the landowner, but by then the relationship between Bill and the Tarmac Properties' management had broken down completely; the company subsequently agreed a deal which enabled the trust's former works' manager, Bill Jefferies, and a Hull businessman, Ken Ryder, to take up a tenancy inside the works.

The pair established a new operation, the Swindon Locomotive Carriage & Wagon Works, which in turn was taken over by engineer Steve Atkins, who rebranded it as Swindon Railway Engineering.

Hawksworth pannier No 9400 arrives at the then new Swindon Railway Museum on 8 April 1962.
PAUL CHANCELLOR COLLECTION

Meanwhile, the original Swindon Heritage Trust remained without a home until 1994 when Bill Parker bought the semi-derelict engine house at Flour Mill Colliery at Bream in the Forest of Dean, a Grade II listed building dating from 1908.

It was restored with the help of a grant from the Rural Development Commission to accommodate the trust, which began operations again, and is still trading under the name of Swindon Railway Workshop, even though its home – the Flour Mill workshops – lies in deepest Gloucestershire, the county next to Wiltshire!

The 'new' Swindon Works' first job, ironically, was overhauling the NRM's replica Gooch broad gauge 4-2-2 *Iron Duke*, which was completed in time for museum's annual dinner in September 1996.

The trust then won the contract to carry out the 10-year boiler overhaul of NRM's replica of Stephenson's *Rocket*; also completed on time to a tight schedule.

Various private owners soon became aware that something was stirring in the forest, and began inquiring about bringing locomotives in for maintenance, repair, or long-term overhaul as and when funds permitted.

Since those early successes, the Flour Mill team has achieved many notable successes, not least of which is the restoration of both surviving London & South Western Railway Beattie well tanks, Nos 30585 and 30587 to running order.

Classic Swindon products overhauled at the works include GWR Hall No 6960 *Raveningham Hall*,

Standard 9F No 92203 and GWR 2-8-0 tank engine No 4247.

The workshop team also completed the rebuilding of GWR 0-6-0 pannier tank No 4612 from little more than a pile of spare parts, frames, a boiler and wheels, two of them with spokes cut, after it was bought from Barry scrapyard and had been used as a 'donor' locomotive to keep sister No 5775 running on the Keighley & Worth Valley Railway. With many new components having to be made from scratch, the finished locomotive, now running on the Bodmin & Wenford Railway, is all but a new Swindon pannier!

The Flour Mill workshops overhauled the boiler for *City of Truro* so it could complete its centenary run in 2004, after retired London banker Alan Moore, a sponsor of the Bodmin & Wenford and other heritage lines and long-time friend of Bill Parker, agreed to pay for the work to be done.

In 1998, Swindon Borough Council publicly launched major plans to turn part of the closed Swindon Works into a major visitor attraction, called STEAM – Museum of the Great Western Railway.

It would replace the existing Swindon Railway Museum in Faringdon Road, which had occupied a building originally designed by the GWR in 1847 as a lodging house for single male employees. Workers, however, did not like the institutionalised regime, and what became known as 'the barracks' was in 1867 sold for conversion to a Wesleyan Chapel.

In 1962, it became the town's first railway museum, housing the 'remade' *North Star*, No 4003 *Lode Star*, Dean Goods No 2516, pannier tank No 9400 and railcar No 4, plus, of course, *City of Truro*.

When STEAM was set up inside a Grade II listed Victorian machine shop in the heart of the redundant works' site at a cost of £13-million, including a substantial contribution from the Heritage Lottery Fund, the Faringdon Road collection was 'relocated' inside.

Today, you can see classics such as No 4073 *Caerphilly Castle*, No 6000 *King George V* and, representing the Barry scrapyard era, unrestored 2-8-0 tank engine No 4248.

The award-winning museum tells the story of Swindon's great works, focusing on the people who worked there: one of the modern exhibits is a 'wall of names' honouring former employees.

Waxwork exhibits demonstrate how employees carried out their daily work in reconstructed offices, stores, workshops, a signalbox, a carriage-building shop and a foundry.

The story of Brunel and his railway is outlined, and there are many hands-on exhibits and interactive displays. Often, former railway workers are on hand to offer visitors a personal insight into many of the exhibits. There are plans to add a live steam-running line in the future.

The museum also holds a massive archive of books, periodicals, photographs, drawings and plans, all relating to the GWR.

STEAM is not only a mine of information but a unique source of inspiration for those who wish to know more about Swindon's illustrious past.

It had been hoped to include the Swindon Railway Engineering business in No 9 Shop as an added attraction, but this has not materialised. Following protracted discussions between Steve Atkins and the owners of the freehold, he was due to quit the premises in 2007 so that they can be turned into more store space for the McArthur Glen Designer Outlet, the shopping mall which has been tastefully set up inside the main part of the restored works' buildings. Opened in March 1997, it is Europe's largest covered designer outlet and attracts three million shoppers each year. Sadly, Brunel's works now sells other manufacturers' products, rather than building its own.

The works' engineers office is now the headquarters of English Heritage, where purpose-built storage houses the archive of the National Monuments Record Office. The National Trust also has its headquarters on the site.

On 12 December 2006, *Heritage Railway* magazine sponsored the movement of the last Swindon-built locomotive to leave Swindon Works – the chassis of GWR 2-8-2 tank engine No 7200, which is under restoration at the Buckinghamshire Railway Centre.

However, it was not to be the last steam locomotive to be outshopped from the works.

That honour went to an old industrial Peckett 0-4-0 saddle tank which had no connection whatsoever with Swindon or the GWR, and which Steve Atkins has restored to running order in the

The frames of GWR 2-8-2 tank engine No 7200, the last main line steam locomotive to undergo engineering at Swindon Works, shortly before their removal back to Buckinghamshire Railway Centre on 12 December 2006. JOHN STRETTON

guise of Welsh engine and star of the children's book and TV series, Ivor the Engine, with the purpose of making it the centrepiece of themed attractions at preserved lines all over the country.

The M5 class Peckett, No 1555 of 1920, which spent its working life in Nottinghamshire, left No 9 Shop by lorry on 2 May 2007, bringing down a curtain on locomotive engineering at Swindon that had first been raised by Brunel and Gooch and lasted for 167 years, from Iron Duke to Ivor.

"I think Brunel and Gooch would have smiled at the idea of Ivor being the last to leave their works," said Steve. ∎

The final word at Brunel's works: industrial Peckett saddle tank became the last engine to leave the last vestige of a commercial engineering workshop on 2 May 2007. SWINDON EVENING ADVERTISER

Bill Parker, the man who reopened part of Swindon works and then 'moved' the business to the Forest of Dean. ROBIN JONES

Dai Woodham's scrapyard

The defining im age of late sixties railways that was Barry scrapyard: rows upon rows of derelict main line steam engines rust in the Bristol Channel air, although most of them found their way into preservation. At the forefront can be seen GWR 0-6-2 tank engine No 5643, which has been restored to running order on the Swindon & Crciklade Railway, and No 7200, which is undergoing long-term restoration at the Buckinghamshire Railway Centre.
PAUL CHANCELLOR COLLECTION

S windon was not only a birthplace for numerous classic locomotives, but it was also their graveyard, where generations of obsolete types met their end at the cutter's torch.

When British Railways began withdrawing steam locomotives en masse during modernisation, their numbers were too great to be handled by existing railway works, and were sold to scrap merchants.

In many cases, locomotives were cut up within a few weeks, often days, of their arrival.

However, one man, Dai Woodham, who ran a scrapyard at Barry in South Wales, had other ideas.

In autumn 1965 he decided to concentrate on cutting up redundant wagons, because that side of the business was more profitable.

He left the rows and rows of main line locomotives that he had bought, to rust at their leisure in the Bristol Channel air.

When the first heritage railways were set up, steam locomotives to run on them were mostly bought straight out of British Railways' service.

However, as more and more steam disappeared from the network, it became increasingly more difficult to obtain suitable examples.

With the upsurge of interest in railway preservation as main line steam died, it was only a matter of time before Woodham's huge collection of scrap engines

came to the attention of the revivalists. Mercifully, he had held off cutting them up for so long that the preservation movement had evolved to the point that it was able to buy the rusting hulks one by one.

Herein lies the reason why the heritage railway portfolio today is 'top heavy' with Swindon products.

When locomotives were withdrawn, they were sent to their nearest scrapyard. Because cutting was undertaken so swiftly elsewhere, other companies such as the London & North Eastern Railway are by comparison poorly represented. Even certain classes of British Railways' Standards only a few years old were rendered extinct.

Out of 213 locomotives bought from Woodhams for preservation purposes, 98 were GWR types, another nine were Swindon-built Standards and two, Stanier 8F No 48431 and Ivatt 2MT No 46512 were built at the works for use elsewhere.

Not all classes appeared at the Barry scrapyard, others being cut up elsewhere. That is why we have today, for instance, 11 Halls, but no Grange nor a Hawksworth County, and lack key classes from other 'Big Four' companies such as an LMS Patriot or a London & North Western Railway Precursor.

Born in 1919 as David Lloyd Victor Woodham, young Dai helped run the family's docks-portering business set up by his great grandfather around the turn of the century. In the late 1930s, the firm looked

to road transport and the scrap metal business, and in 1957 began dismantling railway wagons as a result of the 1955 Modernisation Plan which sought to reduce the British Railways' wagon fleet from 1,250,000 to just 600,000.

In 1958 the BTC decided to speed up the disposal of the steam fleet, while Standard 9Fs were still being built at Swindon.

On 25 March 1959, the first batch of engines was sent to Barry – GWR moguls Nos 5312/60/92/97. In all, 297 engines were sold to Woodhams up to 1968.

The first engine bought from Woodhams was Midland Railway 4F 0-6-0 No 43924, which left Barry in September 1968 and re-entered service on the Keighley & Worth Valley Railway in 1970.

Preservation purchases came at regular intervals, and the 50th to go was GWR prairie No 4144, which left for Didcot in April 1974.

The 10th locomotive saved from Barry quickly went out of existence. Restorers of GWR Hall No 4983 *Albert Hall* eventually found that all was not as it had seemed, and the engine was really No 4965 *Rood Ashton Hall* – the result of an interchange of parts at Swindon in the early 1960s.

Sister No 4936 *Kinlet Hall*, now also based at Tyseley Locomotive Works, may be considered the greatest Barry survivor of all. In 1941, it nearly toppled into a bomb crater following a Nazi air raid on Plymouth after No 4911 became the first of the class to become extinct when it was blown up.

Kinlet Hall left Barry in 1981 and has since returned to the main line.

The 100th locomotive to be restored from Barry scrapyard condition was pannier tank No 9682, which resteamed in January 2000 on the Swindon & Cricklade Railway and is currently at the Chinnor and Princes Risborough Railway.

Miracles have been achieved with the restoration of ex-Barry locomotives.

The scrapyard closed in the late 1980s.

Ten of the last locomotives at Woodhams were bought with public money for cosmetic restoration and display for a planned national railway museum for Wales, earmarked for a site in Cardiff, but the project was later shelved.

They passed into the custody of what is now known as the Barry Island Railway, a three-mile heritage line which runs from Barry Island around Barry Docks and the site of the scrapyard. It serves Woodham's Halt, named after the legendary scrapman, who died from lung cancer on 12 September 1994, and who had been awarded an MBE in 1987 for his business initiatives, which had helped to create many jobs, not for his scrap dealings.

However, his decision not to cut up 213 locomotives has made so much of the preservation movement possible, and allowed future generations to enjoy so many more Swindon masterpieces than would otherwise have been saved.

The 'Barry 10' as they came to be known, comprised GWR 2-8-0 No 2861 (built 1918), 2-6-2T No 4115 (1936), 2-8-0T No 5227 (1924), 2-6-2T No 5539 (1928), 0-6-2T No 6686 (1928), Modified Hall No 7927 *Willington Hall* (1950), LMS 'Black Five' 4-6-0 No 44901 (1945), 8F 2-8-0 No 48518 (1944), BR Standard 4MT 2-6-4T No 80150 and BR Standard 9F 2-10-0 No 92245 (1959). ∎

Heavy freight 2-8-0 No 3862 heads a long line of rusting wrecks at Dai Woodham's scrapyard on 5 March 1968. The locomotive is being restored at the Northampton & Lamport Railway. PAUL CHANCELLOR COLLECTION

Some of the last engines to leave Barry scrapyard for preservation are still to be found in the town, now protected from the elements in this former diesel depot and in the care of the Barry Island Railway, a heritage line which rounds around the northern edge of the late Dai Woodham's premises. ROBIN JONES

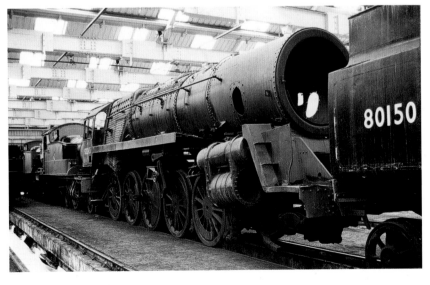

Reclaiming the *main line*

Swindon brings steam back to Britain: the works' most famous locomotive was Collett's King Class 8P 4-6-0 No 6000 *King George V* and the class doyen quickly became an icon to enthusiasts. After withdrawal from BR it devolved into the care of Bulmer, the Hereford cider maker, and during 1971 it became the focus of attention when a tour of Britain was operated to test the prospects of a return to main line action of steam locomotives after a three-year ban. The groundbreaking tour is seen drifting into Severn Tunnel Junction for a water stop on 9 October 1971 as it neared the end of its week long tour on the final stages of its return to Hereford, after which permission was given for limited main line steam activity.
FRED KERR

Despite the mess that had been made of modernising Britain's rail network, with unsatisfactory designs of diesel rushed into production and superb steam engines scrapped when they were just a few years old, the final end came for standard gauge steam haulage with the enthusiasts' 'Fifteen Guinea Special' on 11 August 1968.

After that, British Rail, which proceeded to paint everything it owned in blue or blue and grey, banned steam from the network, apart from trips behind *Flying Scotsman* that had already been promised. On 29 June, it ran a special, from Newcastle-upon-Tyne to Keighley and Carlisle.

The ban was lifted slightly to allow three preserved locomotives, including Castle No 7029 *Clun Castle*, to steam on a length of track at Cricklewood Depot open day in July 1969. However, total prohibition became effective when, later that year, *Flying Scotsman* embarked on an ill-fated tour of North America.

It seemed to everyone that live steam would now be confined to preserved lines, which are allowed to run at a maximum speed of only 25mph.

The Association of Railway Preservation Societies, forerunner of today's Heritage Railway Association, began holding talks with British Rail about relaxing the ban, and a breakthrough came when Richard Marsh became chairman of the British Railways Board in 1971.

A trial 'steam comeback' tour was arranged for early October that year, headed by none other than

the first GWR King, No 6000 *King George V*.

Then owned by Bulmer the cider manufacturer, which had briefly run a steam centre at its Hereford base, *King George V* headed an eight-coach train comprising five Pullman coaches (in Bulmer's green and cream livery) and three British Rail Mark I coaches.

The route of the special included London, Swindon, Newport and Birmingham, and hundreds of thousands of people flocked to the lineside to see it.

It was a triumph for steam, and for Swindon engineering.

As a result, British Rail agreed to open 300 miles of track to steam and approved 23 locomotives for use on them. The Swindon products so approved included *King George V*, No 7029 *Clun Castle*, No 4079 *Pendennis Castle*, panniers Nos 7752 and 7760, prairie No 6106, No 6998 *Burton Agnes Hall*, auto tank No 1466, mogul No 5322, Standard 4MT No 75029 and Standard 9F No 92203.

The first of a series of 'Return to Steam' railtours took place on 10-11 June 1972, when *Clun Castle* made a return run from Tyseley to Didcot.

Many landmarks were to follow in the years ahead as steam reclaimed more and more lost ground.

On 1 March 1979, steam returned to Paddington in the form of *King George V* hauling a special to Didcot.

King George V powers away from Swindon on 31 August 1985. Now a static exhibit inside the town's STEAM museum, as of 2007 there were no plan s to return it to running order again. BRIAN SHARPE

Swindon icon *King George V* at Hereford in April 1976. BRIAN SHARPE

The only preserved Swindon-built diesel currently operating on the main line is D1015 *Western Champion*, seen at Taunton heading a Paignton-bound special for railtour operator Bernard Staite's retirement party on 28 February 2005. ROBIN JONES

As part of celebrations to mark the 150th anniversary of the founding of the GWR, Easter 1985 saw steam running to Plymouth behind *King George V* and No 7819 *Hinton Manor* from Bristol (although the King failed at Taunton). Hall No 4930 *Hagley Hall* and No 7819 *Hinton Manor* hauled the return trip.

Main line steam returned to Cornwall on 6 September 1985 when Clun Castle hauled an excursion from Plymouth to Truro and back.

The haunt of Dukedogs and Manors, steam was back on the Cambrian Coast Line in May behind No 7819 *Hinton Manor*.

In April 2000, *Heritage Railway* magazine broke the news that No 3440 *City of Truro* was to be returned to the main line in time mark the centenary of its unofficial record-breaking run. Indeed, it hauled two 'Ocean Mail 100' specials over Wellington Bank on 8 and 10 May 2004, either side of the actual anniversary, and at nothing like the alleged speed of 1904!

Open access coinciding with the privatisation of British Rail in the early 1990s opened up most of the network to steam haulage, and today several companies offer regular trips.

The biggest trip of them all, and possibly the longest in the history of the rail network itself, never mind preservation, however, came in the form of the King's Lynn-based Railway Touring Company's nine-day steam-hauling 'Land's End to John O'Groats' trip of 6-14 April 2007. Using seven steam locomotives, it was operated by the Carnforth-based West Coast Railway Company, and was hailed as an outstanding success.

Leading the way from Penzance out of the West Country were, appropriately, two Swindon products, Tyseley-based King No 6024 *King Edward I* and Didcot's Castle No 5051 *Earl Bathurst*, making a splendid run over the notorious South Devon banks on the leg to Bristol.

Whereas Didcot has become 'Swindon in exile' because of its GWR stock collection and archives, Tyseley holds a similar position today with regards to overhauling, maintaining and rebuilding GWR locomotives for main line running.

Indeed, there has been a continuous steam presence at Tyseley since the GWR roundhouse was built in 1908 to serve the needs of the growing traffic in and around Birmingham.

In the final years of steam, it temporarily housed locomotives bought for preservation straight out of British Railways' service, including GWR prairie No 4555 and panniers Nos 6435 and 1638, after being bought for the nascent Dart Valley Railway by Midland businessmen Pat Garland and Pat Whitehouse, well remembered for his *Railway Roundabout* films on TV in the 1960s. No 4555, although owned privately, was even used on rush-hour commuter trains from time to time!

When *Clun Castle* was bought for preservation, Pat Whitehouse moved it to Tyseley. It remained there after the shed closed to steam in 1966, along with an

Definitely a non-authentic livery for a Great Western locomotive, the bright red carried by Hall No 5972 *Olton Hall* has made it arguably one of the world's most famous steam locomotives. Built at Swindon in 1937, it was returned to working order from Barry scrapyard condition by David Smith, whose Carnforth, Lancashire-based West Coast Railway Company is today one of Britain's top independent heritage main line operators. As millions of young film addicts will know, the locomotive was contracted to Warner Brothers for big-screen appearances in the movie versions of JK Rowling's Harry Potter series of books, and appears in red as *Hogwarts Castle*. It is seen at York in June 2004. ROBIN JONES

LMS 'outsider' in Jubilee class 4-6-0 No 5593 *Kolhapur*.

During the years of the steam ban, Pat Whitehouse and his preservation team built up a workshop to maintain their locomotives, and ran a series of highly successful open days.

Agreements were made for the revivalists to take over part of the depot, although sadly, by then, the great roundhouse had been demolished. Part of the depot evolved into Birmingham Railway Museum, while the engineering side, which has been under the auspices of chief mechanical engineer Bob Meanley for many years, is known as Tyseley Locomotive Works.

Inside, Swindon classics such as Castle class

No 5080 *Defiant* and Halls No 4965 *Rood Ashton Hall* and No 4953 *Pitchford Hall* have been expertly rebuilt from Barry scrapyard condition.

The next to steam for the first time in the heritage era will be Castle No 5043 *Earl of Mount Edgcumbe*.

Tyseley has its own tours' division, Vintage Trains, which runs steam and heritage diesel-hauled trips from Birmingham over the network. Its flagship operation, however, is the summer Sundays' twice-daily 'Shakespeare Express' which sees Swindon steam running trips from Birmingham to Stratford-upon-Avon and back.

Through Tyseley, the main line spirit of Swindon lives on. ∎

Castle class 4-6-0 No 5051 *Earl Bathurst* and Hall No 4930 *Hagley Hall* proudly display their bursts of Swindon steam as they depar Bristol Temple Meads on 7 July 1985 with the 'Great Western Limited.'
BRIAN SHARPE

***King George V* lines up at its Swindon birthplace as a British Rail High-Speed Train whizzes past on 19 May 1979.** BRIAN SHARPE

RECREATING LOST SWINDON GLORIES

Steam building in the 21st century

The preservation movement was left with an arbitrary assortment of locomotives, many of them acquired by chance rather than through choice. In an ideal world, at least one of each type would have been saved. However, because the early preserved railways did not have the financial resources to pick and choose as key locomotive classes were becoming extinct, or more fittingly, because there were no preservation schemes around at the time, the preservation movement has inherited a steam fleet that is by no means truly representative of British railway history.

Therefore, the only way to tell the whole story, apart from using models and photographic records, is to build new locomotives to fill in the missing gaps.

In 1979, the Ffestiniog Railway unveiled *Earl of Merioneth*, a new 'double Fairlie' locomotive, based on a century-old design and built at its Boston Lodge works, but produced with a modern outline; its purpose to supplement the steam fleet rather than filling any historical void. The same year, the NRM commissioned a working replica of Stephenson's *Rocket* for the Liverpool and Manchester Railway's150th anniversary in 1980. This locomotive has since acted as an ambassador for the museum at events around the world.

It was Swindon technology's turn next to be replicated. For the 1985 GW150 celebrations to mark the 150th anniversary of Brunel's railway, the museum decided to build a fully working replica of broad gauge 4-2-2 *Iron Duke*.

It was made largely using second-hand parts from two Hunslet Austerity 0-6-0 saddle tanks, and cannot therefore be described as a

Standard 3 tank No 82000 in service at Frome in the mid-fifties. An ideal locomotive for a heritage railway today? GWR TRUST COLLECTION

total new build. However, for the first time since June 1893, when the last original broad gauge engines ran (in the form of South Devon Railway 4-4-0 saddle tanks *Leopard* and *Stag*, used at Swindon for shunting stock into the cutting shop for scrapping), people had the opportunity to experience one of the behemoths of Brunel's 7ft 0¼in gauge system.

The new *Iron Duke* was built using modern materials and methods to exactly resemble the 1847 drawings. The most obvious feature placing it in 1847 is the exposed wooden lagging: from 1848 sheet iron covered the lagging and painted to match the tender.

A carriage was built to run behind it, and a short demonstration broad gauge line laid outside the museum so passengers could take a trip back in time to those heady pioneering days.

In late 2007, a new British designed and built express passenger locomotive will steam, in the form of No 60163 *Tornado*, the next of the class of A1 Pacifics designed for the London & North Eastern Railway by Arthur Peppercorn. The 17-year project to recreate an example of the class by the A1 Steam Locomotive Trust will have cost £2.35-million.

However, it will not be the first main line steam locomotive built in Britain since *Evening Star* was rolled out of Swindon works in 1860, unless you conveniently forget broad gauge.

It was at Didcot Railway Centre, home of the

Great Western Society, on 30 April 2005 that the 63rd member of Gooch's groundbreaking Firefly class was launched into service, on the venue's own 7ft 0¼in gauge running line.

The locomotive, a replica of the original *Fire Fly* of March 1840, was the culmination of a project begun by the later Royal Navy Commander John Mosse in Bristol in 1981, using original Gooch drawings from 1839 found in an office in Paddington station. Cmdr Mosse had been working as consultant architect to British Rail on the restoration of Brunel's original Temple Meads station at the time. In 1982, the Firefly Trust was established to built it, and the job was done for less than £200,000, after the project moved by necessity from its headquarters in Bristol to Didcot where construction took place.

The original 62 members of the Firefly class were not built at Swindon, but they paved the way for the GWR to have its own works to turn Gooch's designs into reality and were maintained and repaired there. The new *Fire Fly* perfectly captures the spirit and ambience of the broad gauge era, with its enormous driving wheel, oversize copper domes, stovepipe chimney and wooden boiler cladding. It may look decidedly antiquated, but it was the supersonic jet of its day!

As built, the Firefly class showed from the start that it had the potential to achieve the four targets it had been set: speed, safety, reliability, and ease of maintenance.

Above: The frames and cab for new-build Collett Grange 4-6-0 No 6880 *Betton Grange* on display in the workshops at Llangollen during the hugely-successful Steel, Steam & Stars gala on 20-22 April 2007. ROBIN JONES

Above left: One of the new Hawksworth County driving wheels cast in late winter by William Cook Cast Products Ltd at its Sheffield plant. WILLIAM COOK

Top left: The chimney from Grange No 6868 *Penrhos Grange* has been acquired by the builders of the next in line, No 6880 Betton Grange. ROBIN JONES

The frames of new-build British Railways Standard 3 tank engine No 82045 are unloaded at Eardington on the Severn Valley Railway on 23 April. 82045 FUND

At Didcot, the Firefly Trust plans to build a dedicated engine house on the site complete with water tank, coal stage and pit.

Didcot has emerged as a centre of excellence for creating 'new' locomotives to fill in the voids in the history books, and the Swindon story in particular.

The idea of recreating a member of the legendary Saint class was conceived by Great Western Society member Peter Rich more than 30 years ago, while working on the restoration of Churchward mogul No 5322 at Caerphilly.

His idea stemmed from the GWR's policy of using standard and interchangeable parts for its classes. Although no Saint still existed, one could be created by using parts from rusting GWR engines in the Barry scrapyard, he surmised.

Collett had used No 2925 *Saint Martin* as the basis for his prototype of his Hall class in 1924. So, why not back-convert a Hall, of which several examples survived, into a Saint, to build one for a

fraction of the cost of starting from scratch?

So, in 1973 the Great Western Society purchased No 4942 *Maindy Hall* from Barry scrapyard with the specific intention of using it for a future Saint rebuild. The initial Saint Project was launched in the early 1980s, the intention at that time being to use as many parts as possible from the Hall without alteration. Furthermore, there would be the possibility of converting the locomotive from time to time to run as a similar Churchward Atlantic 4-4-2.

Many components would still need to be made from new. After a major appeal for funding was launched by the society in 1995, money and pledges poured in, allowing a new set of Churchward pattern 6ft 8½in driving wheels to be cast and machined. Both halves of the new cylinder block followed in 1999.

In 2000, *Maindy Hall* was dismantled and the original cylinders and frame extensions were split from the main frame, which was subsequently modified at Ian Riley's engineering workshops at Bury in Lancashire, with extension frames forged, machined and fitted, and returned to Didcot as a rolling chassis in 2006. The last big job that remained in 2007 was the overhaul of the Hall boiler.

The new Saint, which is being built to main line running standards, will be No 2999 *Lady of Legend*.

At the same time, other members of the society were making even bolder plans to resurrect another distinctive Swindon design from the poorly represented Edwardian era – the steam railmotor.

No steam railmotor survived into preservation, leaving a huge void when it comes to telling the story of how the British railway network involved. Designed for branch line use, railmotors effectively featured a carriage with a steam locomotive built into one end, which could be driven from a cab at the rear.

The concept paved the way for the far more successful diesel railcars and mulitple units, leading to today's High Speed Train and Pendolinos. As such, they represent a key bridge link between steam and 'modern' traction.

Railmotors had operated on the Bristol & Exeter Railway as early as 1848 when four vehicles designed by W Bridges Adams ran on the line. Half a century later, other railway companies trialled various designs, including battery-electric and petrol-electric railcars.

Under Churchward, a fleet of 99 railmotors was built between 1904 and 1908.

They were considered successful at first, boosting passenger numbers on many rural lines. However, maintenance proved awkward and required specialist machinery and techniques, and the small locomotives had the power to pull only one other coach, whereas a conventional engine could haul several.

The GWR railmotors were gradually withdrawn between 1914 and 1935, with many of the coach bodies being converted into auto-trailers for push-pull working with locomotives such as Collett's 1400 class.

Among the fleet was No 93, built at Swindon in 1908, and at first allocated to Southall shed. It was later based at Bristol, Croes Newydd, Chalford,

Bottom: GWR steam railmotor No 93 operating on the Clevedon branch. GREAT WESTERN SOCIETY COLLECTION

Below: The original body of railmotor No 93, later auto trailer No 212, on the traverser at Didcot Railway Centre. ADRIAN KNOWLES

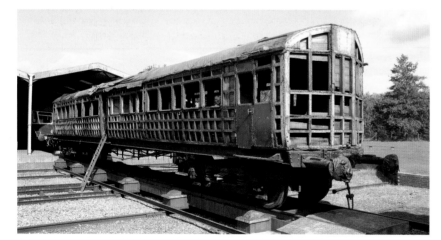

It is not exactly new build, but it is yet an other project the critics said could not be done, and which is now rapidly taking shape at 'Swindon by proxy' otherwise known as Didcot Railway Centre. The Great Western Society bought the rusting remains of King 4-6-0 No 6023 *King Edward I* from Dai Woodham's scrapyard at Barry, despite the fact that driving wheels had already been cut with an oxyacetylene torch. Repalcements for the damaged wheels have been supplied along with a multitude of other new parts, and the society aims to rebuild No 6023 in the single-chimneyed original form of the class. After 1956, Kings were fitted with a double blastpipe and narrower double chimney draughting arrangement, while four-row superheater elements were fitted to give a greater level of superheat. Power soared by 20 per cent speed as a result, and an eight per cent improvement in coal and water consumption was also recorded. As of 2007, all that remained with the restoration of No 6023 was the boiler overhaul. It is planned to run it initially in the experimental blue livery applied by British Railways to main line express passenger engines in the early years of nationalisation before the scheme was abandoned. No 6023 is pictured on the turntable at Didcot in summer 2007. Sioster engine No 6024 *King Edward I* retains the double chimney and blastpipe. ADRIAN KNOWLES

Gloucester, Stourbridge, Taunton and Yatton.

No 93 was condemned as a railmotor at Swindon on 19 November 1934 and was converted into auto-trailer No 212. The auto-trailer was withdrawn from service in May 1956, but rather than being scrapped, it was converted into a 'work study coach' for British Railways and became used as an office in Birmingham.

The Great Western Society bought it in 1970 and brought it to Didcot as the only example of a steam railmotor in preservation.

Plans were hatched to back-convert it to operational condition – by building a new locomotive to run inside it, and the project was formally launched in 1998.

Following years of slow but sure construction of the railmotor's locomotive section, the boiler, built by Israel Newton of Bradford, was steamed for the first time on 11 January 2007. Afterwards it was moved to Tyseley Locomotive Works for trial fitting to its new bogie. An application for major grant aid funding towards the restoration of the coach body and trailer has been made.

When it comes to choosing which classic locomotives to recreate, everyone would have his or her own personal preferences. Would it not be marvellous, for instance, if every enthusiast in Britain agreed to help towards recreating Churchward's *The Great Bear*, for instance? It would never happen.

Each locomotive class has its own devotees, but another new-build scheme, the Three Counties Project, aims to satisfy many by recreating not one but three or more extinct types.

As we have seen, 10 of the last locomotives in Dai Woodham's scrapyard were still together at Barry until fairly recently.

The 'Barry 10' were bought by the now-defunct South Glamorgan Council with £85,000 of grant aid from the former National Heritage Memorial Fund. Numerous inquiries have been made about the rusting hulks by would-be restorers over the years, but the custodians could not dispose of them because of the red tape surrounding the purchase which was made using public money for a specified project.

In 2004, present-day 'owner' the Vale of Glamorgan Council voted in favour of a report by officer John Dent for the release of the 10 locomotives to restoration and new-build schemes, including a plan

to build a new Collett Grange. It has come to be known as the Three Counties Project.

Plans for this project were drawn up by John Buxton of Cambrian Transport Ltd, consultant to both the council and the Welsh Development Agency. Again drawing on the GWR practice of building engines with interchangeable parts, he recommended that some of the 10 could be 'recycled' into extinct locomotive types.

Enough parts could be salvaged to form the basis of schemes to build not only a Hawksworth County 4-6-0, but also the earlier Churchward County 4-4-0 and a largely forgotten design, the 4-4-2 tank engine. There is also serious talk at Didcot of the society also using some parts to help build a Churchward 4700 class 2-8-0 tender locomotive. Thereby filling another gap in preserved railway history.

First to be released from the pool of 'Barry 10' was Hawksworth Modified Hall 4-6-0 No 7927 *Willington Hall*, which on 3 November 2006 was taken by low loader to the Llangollen Railway, home of the 6880 Betton Grange project, which had already made significant strides in its bid to build the next in

The boiler for Great Western Railway steam railmotor No 93 being tested at manufacturer Israel Newton of Bradford on 11 January 2007. ADRIAN KNOWLES

The subframe which will allow new Saint No 2999 to be converted, as required, from a 4-6-0 to a Churchward Atlantic 4-4-2, thereby filling two gaps in preservation.
ADRIAN KNOWLES

line of the 4-6-0s, with a new set of frames cut and machined and many other parts obtained.

At Llangollen, the boiler was lifted off No 7927 and donated to the Grange project. The chassis was then taken away, the frames to be used by the Great Western Society to build a new Hawksworth County – for which a new set of driving wheels were cast in spring 2007, as those from No 7927 are earmarked for use beneath another Hall.

The *Betton Grange* team will remove the three-row superheater from the boiler and carry out a full evaluation of the boiler for its restoration to main line running.

The new County will carry the identity of scrapped No 1014 *County of Glamorgan* in recognition of the council that has allowed the project to happen, and in acknowledgement of its indebtedness to Barry.

The boiler will come from another of the 'Barry 10', Doncaster-built Stanier 8F No 48518. Although an extension to the boiler will be needed, the County and 8F types were otherwise very similar in size.

Both the new Grange and County are expected to cost in the region of £500,000 each to build. Not bad, when you compare them with the cost of the new A1.

The Grange team has embarked on a series of major events to raise both funds and the project's profile. Members were responsible for organising the Steel, Steam & Stars gala at the Llangollen Railway on 20-22 April. Sponsored by *Heritage Railway* magazine and featuring 11 locomotives, mainly Swindon-built types, in action, it raised enough money to build the extension frames. A far bigger event is planned for 2009 to generate money to pay for the biggest item yet to be sourced or made, the cylinder block, as a set of wheels has already been promised.

Meanwhile, a group of Severn Valley Railway footplatemen is making progress with plans to build the next in line of British Railways' Standard Class 3 2-6-2 tanks, as originally built at Swindon.

The project, which was first started by

Buckfastleigh engineman John Besley in 1998, received a boost in 2003 when Stoke-on-Trent City Council agreed to donate a pair of 5ft 3in centre driving wheels from scrapped Standard Class 4MT 4-6-0 No 76080. The wheels are identical to those used on the 82000 class.

In spring 2007, the 82045 Locomotive Fund, as the group is known, took delivery of a new set of machined frames, the first major component to be built for the new locomotive. Other parts have been obtained, and quotes have been invited for the construction of a boiler.

Finally, the West Somerset Railway has taken Swindon steam engineering further forward – by producing a GWR locomotive that never was!

Collett designed a small-boilered 2-6-0, but the type never went into production. The railway had acquired prairie tank No 5193 from Barry scrapyard, but rather than restore 'yet another' 2-6-2T, it decided to add a tender, and create a 'might have been'.

'Normal' moguls had been in regular service on the Minehead branch, so while the rebuild may well be described as 'freelance' to some extent, the type was historically appropriate.

The completed engine made its debut in summer 2004 as No 9351, a rearrangement of its original number, and has to date given excellent service.

*Anyone wishing to contribute to the Betton Grange project or to join the restoration team is urged to write to: Simon Holden, 56 Central Avenue, Birkdale, Southport, Merseyside PR8 3EQ.

Would-be supporters of the County project are invited to send donations to: County 1014 Project, Great Western Society, Didcot Railway Centre, Didcot, Oxfordshire OX11 7NJ.

If you would like to help out with the Saint or steam railmotor, contact Richard Croucher, also at the Didcot address.

Chris Proudfoot of the BR Standard 3 tank project can be contacted by email at ProudfoC@aol.com ∎

The greatest journey
of a Swindon prairie ...

Just when you think it's all over... another chapter in the history of Swindon Works begins. The latest concerns not a GWR King or Castle – but a humble prairie tank, which until early 2007, was an unrestored ex-Barry scrapyard hulk.

That spring, however, it became the first of its type to run passenger trains behind the former Iron Curtain.

The amazing story of prairie No 5521, which spent much of its working life on the Minehead branch, was bought from Woodhams scrapyard for restoration and use on its former home territory of the nascent West Somerset Railway in 1975.

The West Somerset Railway Association, however, realised by the early 1980s that it did not have sufficient funds to restore No 5521, and it was sold Bill Parker and his brother Richard.

Restoration of No 5521 began on the Dean Forest Railway, and when Bill Parker reintroduced heritage engineering back to the old works at Swindon, as we have already seen, it was returned to its birthplace.

There it stayed, receiving little attention, until 1992, when it was evicted by the landlord along with the workshop, and moved to the nearby the Swindon & Cricklade Railway, where it languished for some years under a sheet.

After Bill Parker set up his Swindon Railway Workshop at Bream in the Forest of Dean, No 5521 moved there in 2001 for serious restoration.

As the Bream locomotive repair business went from strength to strength, handling prestigious contracts for NRM among others, the slow restoration of No 5521 took a back seat.

However, on 1 February 2007, No 5521 made the short journey by road from Bream to the nearby Dean Forest Railway, where successfully it ran under its own power the following day.

It subsequently took part in the West Somerset Railway 'Summer Saturdays in the West' spring steam gala, which broke all records by attracting 10,400 passengers.

However, it made its Minehead branch comeback with a decidedly continental appearance as it had been fitted with an air brake, allowing it to haul stock on European main lines.

No 5521 appeared in the centenary celebrations being staged by Wolsztyn steam depot in Poland on 28-29 April, and was given the chance to haul special trains over that country's network.

Wolsztyn is the last bastion of European 'real' steam. A British enthusiast-led initiative, the Wolsztyn Experience, has helped finance the retention of the steam shed and its crews so that foreign visitors can undertake steam-driving experience courses on a genuine, as opposed to preserved, main line.

The prairie was shipped from Hull to Poland via Helsinki, and took part in the celebrations alongside some of the finest preserved steam locomotives from Poland, Germany, Hungary and the Czech Republic. The Wolsztyn Experience organised a day-trip from Gatwick airport for enthusiasts wishing to attend the celebrations, and they were taken to Wolsztyn in a special train hauled by No 5521.

After the centenary event, which included a parade of all the locomotives taking part, No 5521 was coupled behind Hungarian 4-6-0 No 109.109 – and the pair headed another enthusiast special, this time to Budapest.

There, No 5521 went on display in the Hungarian National Railway Museum for the summer. Judging by its sparkling performances on the continent, its adventures are far from over, and neither are those of Swindon's finest. ■

How many times has a German Pacific ever stood side by side with a Swindon-built locomotive in service, let alone a humble prairie tank? FRED KERR

The Stalin-era architecture of Wolsztyn station says it all: Great western Railway small prairie No 5521 has dared to go where none of its class had ever been before. The shunter climbs on to the 1927-built veteran of the Minehead and Bodmin branches as it waits to move off its train on 30 April 2007. FRED KERR

No 5521 makes its individual run in a grand parade of locomotives to mark the centenary of Wolsztyn depot, now, thanks to British enthusiasts, a bastion of 'real' main line steam operations. The prairie may return in 2008 to take charge of scheduled commuter trains from Wolsztyn! FRED KERR

At the Wolsztyn centenary 'carnival of steam', a convoy of seven locomotives returns to the start point, with the prairie in second place. After the event, it headed off under steam to Budapest! FRED KERR